Smoke and Society

The Culture, Consumption, and Control of Tobacco in Mizoram

Smoke and Society

The Culture, Consumption, and Control of Tobacco in Mizoram

Shamim Akhtar

GYAN

Published by

GYAN

Gyan Publishing House
5, Ansari Road
Daryaganj, New Delhi-110002
Phone: 011-47034999, 9811692060
E-mail: books@gyanbooks.com

Distribution Network
gyanbooks.com
India, USA, Canada, UK, Australia, France

ISBN: 978-93-7414-524-1 (PB)
First Published, 2025

Printed at: Gyan Press, Delhi.

Smoke and Society

The Culture, Consumption, and Control of Tobacco in Mizoram

Author: Shamim Akhtar

Dedication

To my parents—

for their unwavering support, quiet sacrifices, and faith in every step of my academic journey.

This work is a reflection of their values, patience, and enduring love.

Contents

Acknowledgement

"If I have seen further, it is by standing on the shoulders of giants."
—Isaac Newton

I am deeply grateful to the Department of Commerce, Mizoram University, for granting me the invaluable opportunity to pursue research in a field that has both intellectually fascinated and emotionally committed me since the beginning of my academic journey. Being accepted into the department's esteemed doctoral programme was a privilege I hold in the highest regard. I owe an immense debt of gratitude to my supervisor, Prof. Laldinliana, whose guidance, encouragement, and profound insights have been pivotal in shaping this research. His mentorship has not only enriched my academic endeavours but will continue to influence my scholarly path for years to come. I also extend my heartfelt thanks to Prof. N.V.R. Jyoti Kumar for his unwavering support and motivation throughout this journey. His consistent guidance, along with the encouragement from the distinguished faculty and fellow scholars of the department, has significantly contributed to my academic and personal growth. Additionally, I am equally thankful to the administrative and support staff of the Department of Commerce, the Central Library, and the Departments of Accounts, Administration, and Examination for their timely and valuable assistance throughout various stages of my research.

I sincerely acknowledge the Mizoram State Tobacco Control Society (MSTC) and Mr. R. Lalremruata, State Consultant, National

Tobacco Control Programme (NTCP) Mizoram, for their valuable support during the course of my research and encouragement towards the publication of this book.

This study would not have been possible without the generous cooperation of those who supported me during my fieldwork at Pachhunga University College and Government Saiha College. I am especially grateful to Dr. Denghmingliani Zadeng, Associate Professor, Department of Mathematics; Dr. Vanlalthana, Assistant Professor, Department of Commerce; Dr. Rualzakhumi Ralte, Associate Professor, Department of English; Dr. Lalthakima, Associate Professor, Department of Political Science; Mr. Zoramkhuma, Assistant Professor, Department of Geography; Dr. Rohmingmawii, Associate Professor, Department of History; Dr. Lalthankungi, Associate Professor, Department of Education; Dr. Emily F. Lalnunpuii, Assistant Professor, Department of Philosophy, all at Pachhunga University College; and Dr. Mark V. Vanlalrema, Assistant Professor, Department of English, Government Saiha College, for their time, help, and thoughtful contributions. I am also deeply thankful to my friends and colleagues at ICFAI University Mizoram for their constant encouragement and moral support, particularly to my dear friend and former colleague, Dr. Pranjal Kalita, whose companionship and motivation have been an enduring source of strength.

No words can adequately express my gratitude to my parents, Abbu and Maa, and my sister, whose unconditional love, patience, and steadfast support have been the foundation of my resilience. Despite the long absences required by academic and professional commitments, they have always stood by me with quiet pride and unwavering belief. I am equally indebted to my in-laws for their constant encouragement, understanding, and support throughout this journey. As I reflect on this path, I remember my late father-in-law, whose untimely passing during the course of my research left an irreplaceable void. To all my family members—each a cherished part of my life—I offer my deepest thanks for their endless love and support.

Finally, to my beloved wife—your patience, sacrifices, and unwavering belief in me have been the cornerstone of this accomplishment. Your support carried me through the most challenging moments of this journey, and for that, I am forever grateful.

To everyone who has walked beside me on this journey—thank you. And to those who will read this book in the future, I deeply appreciate your time, curiosity, and willingness to engage with my work.

Shamim Akhtar

Aizawl

8th May, 2025

Preface

> *"A cigarette is the perfect type of a perfect pleasure. It is exquisite, and it leaves one unsatisfied. What more can one want?"*
>
> — Oscar Wilde

The allure of tobacco lies not in fulfillment, but in the fleeting ecstasy it offers—an ephemeral pleasure that soon gives way to dissatisfaction, guilt, and an intensified craving for more. This cycle of momentary gratification and enduring harm is central to the nature of consumption-related addictions. As the World Health Organisation (WHO) starkly observes, "tobacco is the only legal drug that kills many of its users when used exactly as intended by manufacturers." Responsible for more than 8 million deaths each year—an average of one death every six seconds—and associated with six of the eight leading causes of death globally, tobacco use remains one of the gravest public health challenges of our time. In response, international organisations, government and public health agencies continue their relentless efforts through regulation, awareness campaigns, and social marketing strategies aimed at reducing tobacco addiction and its widespread consequences.

Nestled in the remote northeastern frontiers of India, Mizoram is a small yet culturally vibrant state. It shares domestic borders with Assam, Manipur, and Tripura, and international boundaries with Bangladesh and Myanmar. The state is renowned for its rolling hills, breathtaking landscapes, and a rich cultural heritage that aesthetically blends the spirit of tradition with the promise of modernity. Mizoram was recently recognised as the first state in India to achieve full literacy, recording a literacy rate of 98.20% according to the 2023–24 PFLS survey. Reflecting the overall peaceful and contented life of its people, the India Happiness Report 2020 ranked Mizoram as the happiest state in the country.

Yet, beneath all these glory and picturesque charm lies a troubling reality—escalating rates of drug abuse, alcoholism, and tobacco consumption, particularly among the youth. The early initiation into tobacco use and subsequent addiction have emerged as pressing public health concern for Mizoram. Successive national surveys, including GATS-1 and GATS-2, highlight the severity of the problem, pointing to tobacco use as a significant threat to the health and future of Mizoram's young population.

This book is an outcome and extension of my doctoral research on tobacco consumption behaviour in Mizoram. As part of the study, I conducted a detailed survey of 500 undergraduate students across selected colleges in the state. This demographic was deliberately chosen due to its vulnerability to initiation, experimentation, and habitual use of tobacco. While the sample primarily represents students from specific districts, the findings offer broader insights that may apply to the wider student population across Mizoram. Nevertheless, it is essential to consider the influence of district-wise and institution-specific variations in tobacco control measures, accessibility, and awareness.

Beyond behavioural patterns, this book also explores the wider socio-cultural dimensions of tobacco use in Mizoram. It examines the historical trajectory and current landscape of tobacco control initiatives in the state, assesses the contributions of various stakeholders, and highlights persistent systemic challenges. A significant contribution of this work lies in proposing a context-sensitive social marketing framework tailored to Mizoram's unique cultural and social fabric. Drawing from empirical research and grounded analysis, the book aims to support and strengthen existing tobacco control measures while informing future interventions and policies.

It is my sincere hope that this work contributes meaningfully to the ongoing discourse on public health, policy-making, and social change—ultimately advancing the vision of a healthier, tobacco-free Mizoram.

Chapter - 1

From Habit to Hazard: Introduction to Tobacco Consumption and Control

Around 500 years ago, tobacco was first introduced to the Indian subcontinent. Over time, it evolved into a widely traded commodity and gained widespread acceptance and consumption among the masses. It was soon discovered that many regions of the subcontinent possessed soil and climatic conditions highly favourable for cultivating various types of tobacco. As a result, tobacco became not only a staple for domestic use but also an important export to countries in the West.

The early 20th century marked a turning point with the establishment of the Imperial Tobacco Company of India Limited, a subsidiary of the British American Tobacco Company. This ushered in an era characterised by rapid commercialisation, industrialisation, and the emergence of organised marketing of tobacco and tobacco products in India.

Today, tobacco remains a major public health concern. According to the Global Adult Tobacco Survey (GATS-2) conducted by the Tata Institute of Social Sciences and the Ministry of Health and Family Welfare (TISS & MoHFW, 2018), 28.6 percent—or approximately 266.8 million—of India's adult population (aged 15 years and above) currently use tobacco in some form. Alarmingly, the prevalence is significantly higher in the northeastern states, with Mizoram reporting the second-highest rate in the country: 58.7 percent of its adult population uses tobacco, surpassed only by Tripura.

These sobering statistics compel us to ask several critical questions:

- What are the prevailing trends, patterns, and behaviours of tobacco consumers in Mizoram?
- How do cultural and other contextual factors influence the decision-making process behind tobacco consumption in the state?
- What is the current status and impact of tobacco control initiatives in Mizoram?
- What strategies can be employed to make these control efforts more effective and sustainable?

The chapters that follow will explore these pressing issues in depth, offering insights into the multifaceted nature of tobacco consumption in Mizoram. However, before delving into these discussions, it is essential to establish a foundational understanding of tobacco, its various forms, and the broader context of its consumption. This introductory chapter is therefore dedicated to laying that groundwork.

1.1 Understanding Tobacco: Definitions, Forms, and Chemical Composition

The Cigarettes and Other Tobacco Products (Prohibition of Advertisement and Regulation of Trade and Commerce, Production, Supply and Distribution) Act, 2003, commonly known as COTPA, 2003 (India Code, 2003), provides a comprehensive legal framework for regulating tobacco use in India. According to Section 3(p) of the Act, "tobacco products" include the following:

1. Cigarettes
2. Cigars

3. Cheroots
4. Beedis
5. Cigarette tobacco, pipe tobacco, and hookah tobacco
6. Chewing tobacco
7. Snuff
8. Pan masala or any chewing material containing tobacco as one of its ingredients
9. Gutka
10. Tooth powder containing tobacco

Further, Section 3(b) of the same Act defines a "cigarette" as:

(i) Any roll of tobacco wrapped in paper or in any other substance not containing tobacco;

(ii) Any roll of tobacco wrapped in a substance containing tobacco, which—by reason of its appearance, the type of tobacco used, the filter, or its packaging and labeling—is likely to be offered to, or purchased by, consumers as a cigarette.

This definition explicitly excludes beedis, cheroots, and cigars, even though they may bear similarities in form or function.

The U.S. Food and Drug Administration (FDA) defines "tobacco product" under Section 201(rr) of the Federal Food, Drug, and Cosmetic Act as *"any product made or derived from tobacco that is intended for human consumption, including any component, part, or accessory of a tobacco product"* (Code of Federal Regulations, 2018). This definition encompasses a wide range of items, including cigarettes, cigarette tobacco, roll-your-own tobacco, and smokeless tobacco. Additionally, Section 5702(c) of Title 26 of the United States Code defines tobacco products as *"cigars, cigarettes, smokeless tobacco, pipe tobacco, and roll-your-own tobacco"* (Legal Information Institute [LII], n.d.). Under this statute, smokeless tobacco specifically includes snuff and chewing tobacco (26 U.S.C. § 5702).

Tobacco consumption—whether in smoked or smokeless form—is known to be highly addictive. The 1986 Surgeon General's Report concluded that smokeless tobacco, in particular, is an addictive substance, with dependence potential comparable to that of morphine and cocaine (Henningfield et al., 1997).

Tobacco is produced by processing the leaves of plants belonging to the genus *Nicotiana* (Pain, 2008), most notably *Nicotiana tabacum*, which is widely used for commercial cultivation (Hoof, 2011). The primary psychoactive component of tobacco is nicotine, a substance that acts both as a stimulant and a sedative (Ahmed & Peeran, 2016; Psychology Today, 2019; World Health Organisation [WHO], 2008). Its addictive nature is believed to arise from the interaction between nicotine and monoamine oxidase inhibitors (MAOIs)—specifically beta-carbolines—naturally present in tobacco (Smith et al., 2015). While *Nicotiana tabacum* remains the most common species for tobacco production, other species such as *Nicotiana affinis*, *Nicotiana rustica*, *Nicotiana sanderae*, *Nicotiana alata grandiflora*, *Nicotiana acuminata*, *Nicotiana bigelovii* (Indian tobacco), *Nicotiana longiflora*, *Nicotiana noctiflora*, *Nicotiana suaveolens*, *Nicotiana sylvestris*, and *Nicotiana wigandioides* are also cultivated in various contexts (Kishore, 2014).

Exhibit 1.1: Cultivated Tobacco

Source: https://tobaccoboard.com/

1.2 The Public Health and Socioeconomic Burden of Tobacco Use

Tobacco consumption is a leading global public health crisis, responsible for over 8 million deaths each year—equating to one death every six seconds—and accounting for one in every ten adult fatalities worldwide (WHO, 2019a; HealthHub, 2018). It is implicated in six of the eight leading global causes of death (WHO, 2009a) and is widely recognised as the single most preventable cause of mortality (Australia India Institute, 2012; Reddy et al., 2010; WHO, 2011). If current patterns persist, annual tobacco-related deaths are projected to exceed 8 million by 2030 (WHO, 2008a). Over the past four decades, tobacco use has resulted in an estimated 12 million deaths globally, including 4.1 million from cancer, 5.5 million from cardiovascular diseases, 2.1 million from respiratory illnesses, and approximately 94,000 infant deaths due to maternal smoking during pregnancy (Choudhary, 2001).

Beyond its link to cardiovascular disease and lung cancer, tobacco use is associated with a wide array of other health issues such as various cancers (Bartal, 2001; Mamtani et al., 2017), coronary heart disease, chronic obstructive pulmonary disease (COPD), peripheral vascular disease, stroke, acid peptic disorders (Bartal, 2001), impaired wound healing, cataracts, infertility, premature births, sudden infant death syndrome, and respiratory complications in children born to smokers (Robbins, 2010). Moreover, the use of smokeless tobacco products has been strongly correlated with the high incidence of oral cancers (Office of Medical Applications, 1986).

Globally, there are an estimated 1.3 billion tobacco users, with the vast majority residing in countries with medium levels of human development (Esson & Leeder, 2004). In recent years, the tobacco industry has increasingly shifted its focus from developed to developing countries, where tobacco control policies are often less stringent, presenting opportunities for market expansion (Jatoi et al., 2009; Australia India Institute, 2012). As a result, tobacco use is rising significantly in low- and middle-income nations (Esson & Leeder, 2004). The economic burden of tobacco use on households is equally alarming. In Bangladesh, the amount spent on tobacco could instead feed 10.5 million malnourished children (Efroymson et al., 2001). In Vietnam, the poorest households reportedly spend 2.2 times more on tobacco than on education and 1.6 times more than on healthcare (Efroymson et al., 2011). In countries like Bulgaria, Egypt, Indonesia, Myanmar, and Nepal, low-income households spend between 5% and 15% of their disposable income on tobacco (Esson & Leeder, 2004).

India holds a critical position in the global tobacco economy as the second-largest producer, third-largest exporter (Business Wire, 2019), and second-largest consumer of tobacco (Jhanjee, 2011; WHO India, n.d.). The number of tobacco users in India exceeds the combined population of Indonesia and Canada, making it equivalent in size to the world's fourth-most populous country (Lal et al., 2015). According to the Global Adult Tobacco Survey (GATS) 2016–2017, 28.6% of Indian adults are active tobacco users (TISS & MHFW, 2018). Despite the implementation of tobacco control policies, India continues to bear one of the world's highest burdens of tobacco-related morbidity and mortality (Mohan & Lando, 2016). A historical study estimated that nearly 100 million adults aged 35 and above died prematurely from tobacco use in India between 1910 and 2010 (Lal et al., 2012).

Tobacco use in India reflects a highly complex and diverse pattern influenced by regional, demographic, socio-economic, and cultural factors (Lal et al., 2015). The variety of tobacco products consumed in the country is broader than in most parts of the world, leading to additional public health challenges such as high rates of oral cancer due to widespread use of smokeless tobacco (McKay et al., 2015; Shimkhada & Peabody, 2003). Exhibit 1.2 presents the percentage distribution of tobacco users in India.

In addition to the direct consumption of tobacco—whether through smoking or smokeless forms—which places users at significant risk of various illnesses and serious health conditions (Reddy & Gupta, 2004), exposure to secondhand smoke (SHS) is also associated with a wide array of severe health consequences. These include heart disease, lung cancer (Ghany, 2006), nasal sinus cancer, middle ear infections, asthma, other respiratory illnesses (Robbins, 2010), childhood respiratory infections (Mathew et al., 2011), tuberculosis (WHO, 2018a), and pregnancy-related complications (Do et al., 2018).

Exhibit 1.2: Percentage of Tobacco Users in India

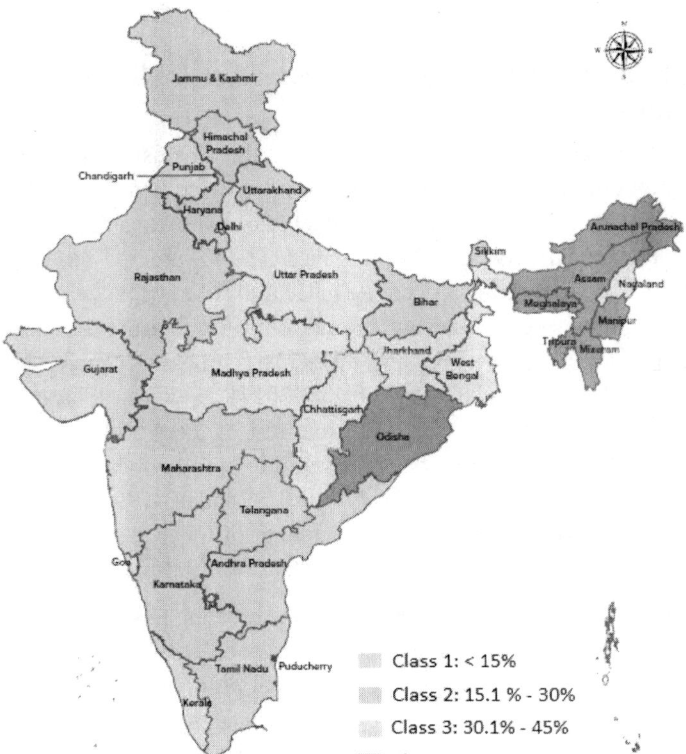

Source: GATS 2 India, 2016-17.

It is also worth noting that despite the well-established negative health impacts of tobacco use, there are historical and cultural accounts of its medicinal application in various traditional systems around the world (Arowolo, 2015; Pain, 2008). However, many of these claimed medicinal uses remain scientifically unverified and require rigorous research and clinical validation (Pain, 2008).

In conclusion, tobacco consumption in its current forms presents a critical public health crisis in India, with far-reaching implications that span health, social, economic, and ethical dimensions. Alarmingly, tobacco use in India continues to rise despite the existence of tobacco control policies (Mohan et al., 2018), highlighting the urgent need for more effective and context-sensitive interventions.

1.3 The Journey of Tobacco: From Sacred Plant to Global Industry

The term *tobacco* originates from the Spanish word *tabaco* (Crawford, 1852). Tobacco plants were first cultivated by Native Americans around 6000 BCE. Artifacts from the Mayan civilisation, which thrived between 2000 BC and AD 900, provide the earliest recorded evidence of tobacco use in Central America (Gately, 2001). Indigenous peoples used tobacco not only for pleasure, but also in religious ceremonies and for medicinal purposes (Gately, 2001; Holmes, 1923; Randall, 1999; Sadik, 2014). However, tobacco and its uses were largely unknown to the rest of the world until 1492, when Christopher Columbus received dried tobacco leaves as a gift from Native Americans (Gately, 2001; Randall, 1999; Reddy & Gupta, 2004). This marked the beginning of tobacco's introduction to Europe.

By around 1531, Europeans began cultivating tobacco in Central America (Tobacco-Free Life, 2016). Its popularity grew rapidly as many Europeans believed in its medicinal properties (Gately, 2001; Holmes, 1923; Randall, 1999). In 1571, Spanish physician Nicolas Monardes claimed in his writings that tobacco could cure 36 ailments (Randall, 1999). During the following century, tobacco became a major trade commodity and was widely used as a cash crop (Jenner, 2014). European physicians even published treatises praising its health benefits (Charlton, 2004). In 1614, tobacco shops began operating across Britain, primarily selling Virginia blend tobacco (Tobacco-Free Life, 2016).

Despite its popularity, tobacco also faced criticism. King James I of England condemned tobacco in his 1604 treatise *A Counterblast to Tobacco*, and in 1624, Pope Urban VIII banned its use in sacred places (Borio, 2001). Between 1633 and 1647, the Ottoman Empire imposed the death penalty for tobacco use (Borio, 2001). By the mid-17th century, European settlers had introduced tobacco cultivation to Africa (Tobacco-Free Life, 2016).

In the Americas, the first tobacco companies were established in Virginia around 1730 (Borio, 2001). In 1760, Pierre Lorillard founded a company in New York City to produce tobacco products such as cigars and snuff (Borio, 2001). Philip Morris began selling hand-rolled Turkish cigarettes in Britain in 1847 (Borio, 2001), and J.E. Liggett and Brother was founded in St. Louis in 1849 (Borio, 2001). By 1861, the first American cigarette factory was producing 20 million cigarettes annually; this number had risen to 4 billion by 1890 (Tobacco-Free Life, 2016). In 1902, British company Philip Morris established its U.S. headquarters in New York to sell brands like Marlboro (Borio, 2001). By 1924, cigarette sales in the U.S. had reached 73 billion units (Borio, 2001).

The marketing of tobacco to women began in the 1920s, with Philip Morris and the American Tobacco Company specifically targeting female consumers. As a result, the number of teenage female smokers tripled between 1925 and 1935 (Randall, 1999). Tobacco's popularity was also reinforced during wartime—during World War I, cigarettes were known as "soldiers' smoke," and in World War II, they were included in soldiers' rations. Many tobacco companies donated millions of free cigarettes to troops, effectively cultivating lifelong customers (Randall, 1999).

The first known link between smoking and lung cancer was proposed in 1912 by Dr. Isaac Adler (Borio, 2001). In 1947, a chemist at Lorillard acknowledged evidence suggesting smoking causes cancer (Tobacco-Free Life, 2016). This was further substantiated in 1967 by Surgeon General William H. Stewart's report, which confirmed the connection between smoking, lung cancer, and heart disease (Borio, 2001).

From the 1970s through the 1990s, tobacco companies faced increasing lawsuits and regulatory restrictions on advertising and marketing. Many began diversifying their portfolios—for instance, Philip Morris acquired the Miller Brewing Company, and RJ Reynolds rebranded as RJ Reynolds Industries, investing in unrelated sectors such as transportation, energy, and consumer goods (Alonso, 1988). In 1996, researchers discovered that tobacco damages a cancer-suppressor gene (Borio, 2001). A landmark moment came in 1997 when Bennett Lebow, CEO of a tobacco company, admitted under oath that cigarettes cause cancer (Levin & Stolberg, 1997).

From the 1990s onward, governments and international bodies initiated comprehensive efforts to curb tobacco use through legislation—banning smoking in public places and restricting advertising. By the 1980s and 1990s, major tobacco companies began shifting their focus away from Western markets to expand aggressively into developing countries in Asia, where regulatory environments were less stringent (Randall, 1999).

Tobacco was first introduced to India by Portuguese sailors through the coast of Goa in the 16th century (Kishore, 2014; Reddy & Gupta, 2004; Shimkhada & Peabody, 2003). Initially, it was cultivated in the Kaira and Mehsana districts of Gujarat (Chikkala, 2014). An interesting anecdote surrounds the invention of the hookah: when Portuguese visitors offered tobacco to Emperor Akbar, there was concern in his court regarding the safety of inhaling an unfamiliar substance. The royal hakim proposed that the smoke be filtered through water to make it safer, leading to the creation of the hookah (Chadda & Sengupta, 2002; Chattopadhyaya, 2000; Soni, 2012). By 1610, tobacco had become a mass phenomenon, widely used across various socio-economic and gender groups (Bhonsle et al., 1992; Soni, 2012). The Indian subcontinent proved highly suitable for the cultivation of different varieties of tobacco, making India not only self-sufficient in tobacco production but also a significant exporter to European countries.

In 1901, the British and American Tobacco Company expanded its operations in India, and by 1906, three of its ventures merged to form the Imperial Tobacco Company, the first Indian cigarette manufacturing firm (Reddy & Gupta, 2004). During the 1930s, other cigarette companies emerged, including the Vazir Sultan Tobacco Company Limited in Hyderabad and the Golden Tobacco Company in Bombay, both founded in 1930, and the Godfrey Cigarette Manufacturing Company in Delhi in 1936 (Chikkala, 2014).

To support tobacco cultivation, the Indian Central Tobacco Committee (ICTC) was established in 1945. It later founded the Central Tobacco Research Institute in 1947 to undertake research on tobacco and cigarettes (Reddy & Gupta, 2004). In 1956, the Tobacco Export Promotion Council (TEPC) was created to promote tobacco exports, followed by the establishment of the Directorate of Tobacco Development in 1966 to monitor production, trade, marketing, and consumption of tobacco in India (Reddy & Gupta, 2004). To further regulate production and address imbalances in supply and demand, the Government of India enacted the Tobacco Board Act of 1975, replacing the TEPC. The Tobacco Board, headquartered in Guntur, Andhra Pradesh, was officially constituted on January 1, 1976 (Chikkala, 2014). Its stated mission is "to strive for the overall development of tobacco growers and the Indian Tobacco Industry" (Tobacco Board, 2014).

India is currently the second-largest producer of tobacco globally, with an estimated annual production of 800 million kilograms. It also ranks as the third-largest producer of Flue-Cured Virginia (FCV) tobacco, a variety commonly used in cigarettes. Remarkably, this level of production is achieved using only about 0.24% of the country's total cultivated land (The Tobacco Institute of India, n.d.). In the fiscal year 2023–24, tobacco and its related products contributed around ₹12,005.89 crore in foreign exchange earnings to the national exchequer (Tobacco Board, 2025).

1.4 The Beginning of ENDS: Disrupting Traditional Tobacco

Though traditional methods of nicotine consumption through tobacco products remain popular, newer alternatives such as electronic nicotine delivery systems (ENDS)—including e-cigarettes—are increasingly gaining ground. In 2024, e-cigarettes emerged as the most widely used tobacco product among middle and high school students in the United States (Jamal et al., 2024). The *World Health Organization's Report on the Global Tobacco Epidemic 2021* highlights the challenges posed by these emerging tobacco products, including ENDS and heated tobacco products (WHO, 2021). The rise in demand for such non-combustible products is often attributed to declining cigarette sales in several countries and the enforcement of smoke-free laws (Agaku & Ayo-Yusuf, 2014). Over the past decade, e-cigarettes and other ENDS have become widely available in global markets.

Exhibit 1.4: Type of Electronic Cigarette Products

Product	Description	Some Brands
Disposable e-cigarette 	Cigarette-shaped device consisting of a battery and a cartridge containing an atomizer to heat a solution (with or without nicotine). Not rechargeable or refillable and is intended to be discarded after product stops producing aerosol. Sometimes called an e-hookah.	NJOY OneJoy, Aer Disposable, Flavorvapes
Rechargeable e-cigarette 	Cigarette-shaped device consisting of a battery that connects to an atomizer used to heat a solution typically containing nicotine. Often contains an element that regulates puff duration and /or how many puffs may be taken consecutively.	Blu, GreenSmoke, EonSmoke
Pen-style, medium-sized rechargeable e-cigarette 	Larger than a cigarette, often with a higher capacity battery, may contain a prefilled cartridge or a refillable cartridge (often called a clearomizer). These devices often come with a manual switch allowing to regulate length and frequency of puffs.	Vapor King Storm, Totally Wicked Tornado
Tank-style, large-sized rechargeable e-cigarette 	Much larger than a cigarette with a higher capacity battery and typically contains a large, refillable cartridge. Often contains manual switches and a battery casing for customizing battery capacity. Can be easily modified.	Volcano Lavatube

Source: Grana et al. (2014).

According to Grana et al. (2014), electronic cigarettes are devices that deliver a nicotine-containing aerosol (commonly referred to as vapor) by heating a solution typically composed of propylene glycol or glycerin, nicotine, and flavoring agents. While the concept of e-cigarettes dates back to 1965 (Lichtenberg, 2017), the first commercially successful version emerged in China in 2003. These devices were subsequently introduced in Europe in 2006 and in the United States in 2007 (CASAA, n.d.; Lichtenberg, 2017). As per projections by Euromonitor International, the global e-cigarette market is expected to grow 17-fold by 2030 (Rawat, 2019).

In India, e-cigarettes were introduced roughly a decade ago and rapidly gained popularity, particularly among the youth (Yadav, 2019). Although ENDS are often marketed and perceived as safer alternatives to conventional cigarettes—due to the absence of smoke and a presumed reduction in respiratory harm (Foulds et al., 2003)—there is considerable debate over their effectiveness and safety as harm-reduction tools (Zatoński & Stokłosa, 2017).

Some research suggests that e-cigarettes contain lower levels of toxic substances compared to combustible cigarettes (Goniewicz et al., 2014), and there is limited evidence that intensive use might aid in cessation efforts (Biener & Hargraves, 2014). However, other studies argue that e-cigarette users may still face comparable risks of lung disease and cancer as traditional smokers (Yadav, 2019). Moreover, these products often contain harmful substances such as lead, cadmium, nickel, formaldehyde, and various hydrocarbons (Lichtenberg, 2017), which raise serious health concerns.

ENDS manufacturers commonly promote their products as 'less harmful' alternatives that can be consumed in smoke-free zones, thereby appealing to a broader consumer base (Yadav, 2019). Yet, as Nguyen and Aamodt (2019) assert, there is currently no robust scientific evidence to support the claim that e-cigarettes serve as effective substitutes for smoking cessation. In fact, a number of studies have shown that ENDS users are likely to become dual users—consuming both e-cigarettes and traditional cigarettes (Agaku et al., 2013; Pearson et al., 2012; Yadav, 2019). There is also evidence suggesting that use of such alternative products may act as a gateway to conventional smoking, especially among youth (Dutra & Glantz, 2014; Klesges et al., 2010; Leventhal et al., 2015).

In response to these emerging threats, the Government of India has taken a strong stance against ENDS. On the recommendation of the Indian Council of Medical Research (ICMR), which cited the precautionary principle in public health, the government announced a complete prohibition on e-cigarettes. On September 18, 2019, it introduced the *Prohibition of Electronic Cigarettes (Production, Manufacture, Import, Export, Transport, Sale, Distribution, Storage and Advertisement) Ordinance, 2019* (Rawat, 2019). The Act came into force on 5th December 2019 through its official notification in the Gazette of India. However, despite the ban, young people in India seem to have little difficulty accessing vapes and e-cigarettes, which are readily available through both online and offline platforms (Puri, 2025). Recent media reports have also highlighted the alarming trend of rising vaping among Indian teenagers, even as the use of traditional cigarettes continues to decline (Clarance, 2025).

Moreover, public health experts caution that the greater threat may lie not in current e-cigarettes alone, but in the emergence of more advanced nicotine delivery technologies. According to Greg Connolly, the next generation of products—such as Marlboro's IQOS or R.J. Reynolds' VUSE FOB—pose an even greater risk. These devices combine drug delivery systems with smartphone-like features, internet connectivity, and digital marketing capabilities, enabling customized nicotine delivery for users (Zatoński & Stokłosa, 2017).

1.5 Tobacco Marketing vs. Tobacco Control: The Ongoing Battle

Tobacco consumption is strongly influenced by the extensive spending on advertising and promotional efforts by the tobacco industry. Research consistently shows that increased exposure to tobacco marketing leads to higher tobacco consumption (Agaku & Ayo-Yusuf, 2014; Brown & Moodie, 2009; Dube et al., 2013; Mohan & Lando, 2016; Pierce & Gilpin, 1995). Even brief exposure to tobacco advertising among young people can foster favourable perceptions about smoking (Evans et al., 1995). Studies have found that students exposed to tobacco advertising at more than four locations are 1.5 times more likely to begin using tobacco than those who are not exposed (Arora et al., 2012a). The marketing tactics of the tobacco industry can even create conditions that encourage youth to illegally purchase tobacco (Widome et al., 2012). Exposure to retailer-level tobacco advertising has been associated with early initiation into tobacco use among adolescents (Feighery et al., 2006; Henriksen et al., 2010; MacFadyen et al., 2001; Slater et al., 2007; Wakefield et al., 2006), continued youth smoking (Kim et al., 2013), relapse among former smokers (Kirchner et al., 2013), and unplanned cigarette purchases (Carter et al., 2009). Moreover, the tobacco industry has been accused of leveraging youth-oriented platforms, such as social media, to promote their products (Freeman & Chapman, 2010). In several Asian countries where smoking among women is culturally deemed inappropriate, tobacco companies target young women by associating smoking with independence, stress relief, and weight control (Kaufman & Nichter, 2001).

As mentioned earlier, due to increasing restrictions on tobacco marketing in Western countries, many Western tobacco companies shifted their focus to markets outside the U.S. and Europe, gaining significant ground in developing and underdeveloped countries in Asia (Randall, 1999). Cussen and McCool (2011, p. 70) pointed out that "low and lower-middle income countries are acutely vulnerable to exploitation by the tobacco industry." The U.S. National Cancer Institute and WHO (2016, p. 258) further stressed that tobacco companies engage in various marketing activities, ranging from traditional advertising, promotions, and sponsorships to emerging marketing strategies in the digital realm. These activities disproportionately affect vulnerable populations, such as young people and women, particularly in low- and middle-income countries, where these groups are especially susceptible to such efforts.

The tobacco industry's growing influence and market power, particularly in densely populated and underdeveloped regions, necessitate greater global cooperation and more comprehensive tobacco control measures. The WHO Framework Convention on Tobacco Control (WHO FCTC), the first global health treaty on tobacco control, was negotiated under the auspices of the WHO and calls for member states to implement comprehensive measures targeting both the demand for and supply of tobacco products, while counteracting the influence of the tobacco industry and promoting international cooperation for global action (WHO, 2009a). Despite being an early adopter of the WHO FCTC guidelines, India continues to face significant challenges in controlling tobacco consumption due to the powerful marketing tactics of the tobacco industry.

While there are numerous factors influencing tobacco use, the marketing techniques employed by the tobacco industry remain one of the most potent drivers of consumption (Hastings & Saren, 2003). As Hoek (2011, p. 245) aptly noted, "From their members' development and use of profoundly evocative and aspirational imagery to their ability to harness and exploit emerging media, the tobacco industry demonstrates the power of marketing to sell toxic products in the pursuit of profit." In India, the persistent influence of the tobacco industry through creative and innovative marketing practices represents a significant hurdle to effective tobacco control. Although these tactics may not always be overtly visible, they remain a powerful force that undermines India's tobacco control efforts. Over time, tobacco companies have become adept at circumventing legal barriers and demonstrating that it is possible to maintain and expand markets using well-established marketing principles.

Tobacco marketers have skillfully applied the basic 4Ps of the marketing mix—product, price, place, and promotion—to advance their business goals and render tobacco control measures ineffective.

Product Strategies

Tobacco marketers employ a range of product strategies, including brand stretching (Jhanjee, 2011), brand extension into non-tobacco products (Jhanjee, 2011; Reddy & Gupta, 2004), and the introduction of complementary products intended for use with tobacco. By using the same brand name for non-tobacco products, tobacco companies effectively bypass the advertising restrictions imposed by the Cigarettes and Other Tobacco Products Act (COTPA) of 2003. According to consumer behaviour theory, the concept of associative networks in memory suggests that related information is linked in people's minds, so when one piece of information is activated, it can trigger related associations. This psychological principle behind "brand extensions" enables tobacco companies to circumvent the ban on tobacco advertising by using the same brand name for non-tobacco products. Moreover, by packaging pan masala and zarda (used together as a single product) in separate sachets, tobacco marketers can evade advertising bans and promote their brand through various media, including television, billboards, and social media. This tactic also allows them to sidestep the requirement for mandatory pictorial health warnings, which must cover 85 percent of the front and back of tobacco packaging. The introduction of newer products like Electronic Nicotine Delivery Systems (ENDS) further exemplifies the tobacco industry's ability to adapt and explore areas not sufficiently addressed by existing legal frameworks.

Pricing Strategies

Tobacco control through taxation in India has proven to be less effective than desired, primarily due to complexities in the tax system, which tobacco marketers have exploited in their pricing strategies. As a result, many tobacco products, except for branded cigarettes, remain affordable to lower-income groups. While high taxes on cigarettes make them unaffordable for many consumers, tobacco companies rely on rising income levels to offset the price increases, which ultimately leads to greater consumption (Business Wire, 2019). John et al. (2010) suggested that increased consumer income could lead to a more than proportional increase in cigarette consumption. However, Gupta (2006) argued that taxes on tobacco products in India remain low and are not effectively collected for products other than cigarettes, making them accessible even to school children. Gupta further pointed out that the proportion of taxes relative to the retail price of a cigarette pack is significantly lower in India compared to other countries. According to Jhanjee (2011), tobacco taxation in India is discriminatory, covering only the organised sector and being applied inconsistently. John et al. (2010, p. 14) remarked, "Taxation of tobacco products in India is complicated by a myriad of tax structures, loopholes, exemptions, different collection systems, and other challenges of tax administration."

Distribution Strategies

Tobacco marketers also employ extensive distribution strategies, ensuring that cigarettes are available at strategically targeted locations, such as nightclubs, bars, social events, and kiosks. In 2017, Philip Morris International faced allegations for placing Marlboro cigarette advertisements at tobacco shops and distributing free cigarettes at nightclubs and bars to promote the brand (Kalra, 2017; Kalra et al., 2017). These locations, referred to as Legal Age Meeting Points (LAMPs), serve as key distribution hubs for tobacco products (Kalra et al., 2017). Distribution plays a crucial role in the tobacco industry's marketing power. ITC, India's leading cigarette manufacturer (Statista, 2021), has built a robust distribution network across the country. Strand et al. (2004, p. 10) argued that the availability of products through effective distribution offers a significant competitive advantage for "bad" products, which can undermine social marketing efforts promoting "good" behaviour.

Promotional Tactics

Tobacco marketers use a range of promotional tactics, from point-of-sale displays, such as advertising in kiosks (Kalra et al., 2017), to direct promotions targeted at retailers, as well as indirect promotions through films (Arora et al., 2012b; Chadda & Sengupta, 2002; Mishra et al., 2005) and surrogate advertising (Business Wire, 2019). A notable case of surrogate advertising occurred in 2016, when Pierce Brosnan appeared in an advertisement for an Indian pan masala brand, despite pan masala being designed for consumption with tobacco. Brosnan later clarified that he had been misled by the company, which failed to disclose the true nature of the product (Financial Express, 2018). This case underscores the manipulative strategies adopted by tobacco companies. Additionally, violations of point-of-sale advertising provisions, such as reducing the required area for health warnings on packaging, are common (Jhanjee, 2011). Sponsoring events to reinforce brand recognition among vulnerable target groups is yet another strategy used by the industry (Jandoo & Mehrotra, 2008; Jhanjee, 2011).

The combination of these strategies has led to the continued success of the tobacco industry in India, despite efforts to control tobacco consumption through legal and regulatory measures. The persistence of these creative marketing practices poses a significant challenge to the effectiveness of India's tobacco control programme.

* * * *

In conclusion, while regulatory measures and social marketing have proven effective in reducing tobacco use in many parts of the world, India's battle with tobacco control highlights the immense challenge posed by the tobacco industry's creative and continuously evolving marketing strategies. Despite India's early commitment to tobacco control through its adoption of the WHO Framework Convention on Tobacco Control (FCTC) guidelines, the country's efforts have struggled against the powerful and resource-rich tobacco corporations. The industry's ability to circumvent existing regulations through innovative strategies—such as brand extensions, surrogate advertising, creative distribution tactics, and pricing strategies—has made much of the legislative framework ineffective.

Tobacco companies have demonstrated a remarkable capacity for exploiting legal loopholes and regulatory gaps, particularly in low- and middle-income countries like India. These companies continue to target vulnerable populations, especially youth and women, through both traditional and emerging media, including social media platforms. Additionally, the pricing strategies employed by tobacco marketers ensure that tobacco products remain affordable for lower-income groups, which further exacerbates the challenge.

Despite the extensive control measures such as advertising bans, high taxation, and point-of-sale restrictions, the tobacco industry's marketing machinery remains a powerful force. Tobacco marketers continue to rely on manipulative tactics to reinforce brand loyalty, expand market reach, and circumvent legal provisions, effectively stalling the success of India's tobacco control programme. This persistent "game of catch-up" between lawmakers and the tobacco industry underscores the need for more robust and adaptive regulatory frameworks that can address the evolving nature of tobacco marketing.

Ultimately, India's experience reveals that effective tobacco control cannot be achieved through fragmented regulatory measures alone. A more comprehensive, multi-faceted approach that combines stronger legislation, continuous monitoring, and global cooperation is essential for curbing the influence of the tobacco industry and reducing tobacco consumption. Until such an integrated approach is implemented, the battle for effective tobacco control will remain an ongoing and uphill struggle.

* * * *

Chapter - 2

Regional Realities: Tobacco Use in India, Northeast, and Mizoram

Tobacco consumption is a significant public health challenge, both globally and in India. While extensive research has been conducted worldwide on the prevalence, causes, and consequences of tobacco use, as well as on strategies to combat it, similar studies in India have become more robust only in recent decades. National surveys on tobacco use in India have been available since 1995-1996, and these have been further supplemented by specialised tobacco-focused surveys introduced after the establishment of the Global Tobacco Surveillance System (GTSS). This system, developed by the WHO, CDC, and CPHA, enables countries to monitor tobacco use through tools like the Global Youth Tobacco Survey (GYTS), the Global Adult Tobacco Survey (GATS), and others.

The following section of this chapter delves into these national surveys, alongside other relevant literature, to provide an overview of the patterns of tobacco consumption in India. Particular attention is given to the unique tobacco consumption trends in Northeast India and Mizoram. Through this, the chapter offers a comprehensive look at the prevalence and patterns of tobacco use in these regions, highlighting the insights and challenges in tobacco control.

2.1 Tobacco Consumption in India: Trends, Patterns, and Challenges

Tobacco consumption in India is a complex and multifaceted issue, largely due to the diversity in the forms of tobacco products used and the resulting burden of tobacco-related diseases and mortality (Gupta & Ray, 2004b). Patterns of use vary widely across states and regions (Singh & Ladusingh, 2014), and tobacco is consumed in numerous forms including cigarettes, beedis, hookah, cigars, pipes, khaini, gutkha, zarda, paan masala, among others (Shimkhada & Peabody, 2003; Soni, 2012). This widespread and culturally embedded consumption poses a growing threat to public health—particularly among adolescents. Peer pressure, familial exposure, affordability, and easy accessibility are key factors contributing to early initiation and eventual addiction (Soni, 2012).

The first nationally representative household survey on tobacco consumption in India was the 52nd National Sample Survey conducted by the NSSO in 1995–96. It reported that 51.3% of men and 10.35% of women used tobacco in some form (Jandoo & Mehrotra, 2008; Jhanjee, 2011). The NFHS-3 (2005–06) showed slightly higher prevalence, with 57% of males and 11% of females (aged 15–49) using tobacco (Jhanjee, 2011).

Notably, Northeast India—particularly Mizoram—emerges as a region with significantly high tobacco use. According to the India GSPS 2006, 42% of school personnel in the Northeast reported tobacco use on school premises, despite tobacco-free policies being in place in 37.3% of schools. Additionally, 34.3% used smokeless tobacco and 30.2% smoked cigarettes—the highest rates recorded among school staff nationwide (Sinha, 2006). The GYTS 2006 further revealed alarming figures for early initiation: 44.9% of smokers in the region began smoking before age 10. Among students aged 13–15, 18.2% were cigarette smokers, and 20.7% used other tobacco products—the highest rates in India (Sinha, 2006).

The Global Adult Tobacco Survey (GATS), India's most comprehensive tobacco-specific survey, has been conducted in two rounds—2009–10 and 2016–17. The first round was undertaken by the International Institute for Population Sciences (IIPS), and the second by the Tata Institute of Social Sciences (TISS), both on behalf of the Ministry of Health and Family Welfare, with technical support from the World Health Organisation (WHO), Centers for Disease Control and Prevention (CDC), and other partners. GATS employed a multi-stage sampling strategy, interviewing adults aged 15 and above. The first round completed 69,296 interviews (91.8% response rate), and the second round 74,037 interviews (92.9% response rate) (WHO, 2018b). As of May 2025, the third round of the Global Adult Tobacco Survey (GATS-3) in India is in the preparatory phase. The International Institute for Population Sciences (IIPS) has initiated the process of selecting field agencies, and fieldwork is scheduled to be conducted across all 28 states and 8 union territories of India during 2024–25. However, no official release date for the GATS-3 data has been announced yet (IIPS, 2025).

Key Findings from GATS 2 (2016–17):

1. **Tobacco Use**: 28.6% of adults (266.8 million) currently use tobacco—42.4% of men and 14.2% of women. Smokers constitute 10.7% (99.5 million) of adults—19.0% of men and 2.0% of women. Smokeless tobacco use stands at 21.4% (199.4 million)—29.6% of men and 12.8% of women.
2. **Cessation**: 55.4% of smokers and 49.6% of smokeless users intended to quit. However, only 48.8% of smokers and 31.7% of smokeless users reported being advised by a healthcare provider to do so.
3. **Secondhand Smoke**: 38.7% of adults were exposed to secondhand smoke at home, and 30.2% at the workplace. Exposure in restaurants was reported by 7.4%.
4. **Media Exposure**: 19.2% and 18.3% of adults noticed advertisements for smoking and smokeless tobacco respectively. Conversely, 68.0% and 59.3% were exposed to anti-tobacco messaging via TV or radio.
5. **Knowledge and Perceptions**: 92.4% and 95.6% of adults believed that smoking and smokeless tobacco use, respectively, cause serious illness.

Exhibit 2.1: Comparison of GATS 1 & GATS 2

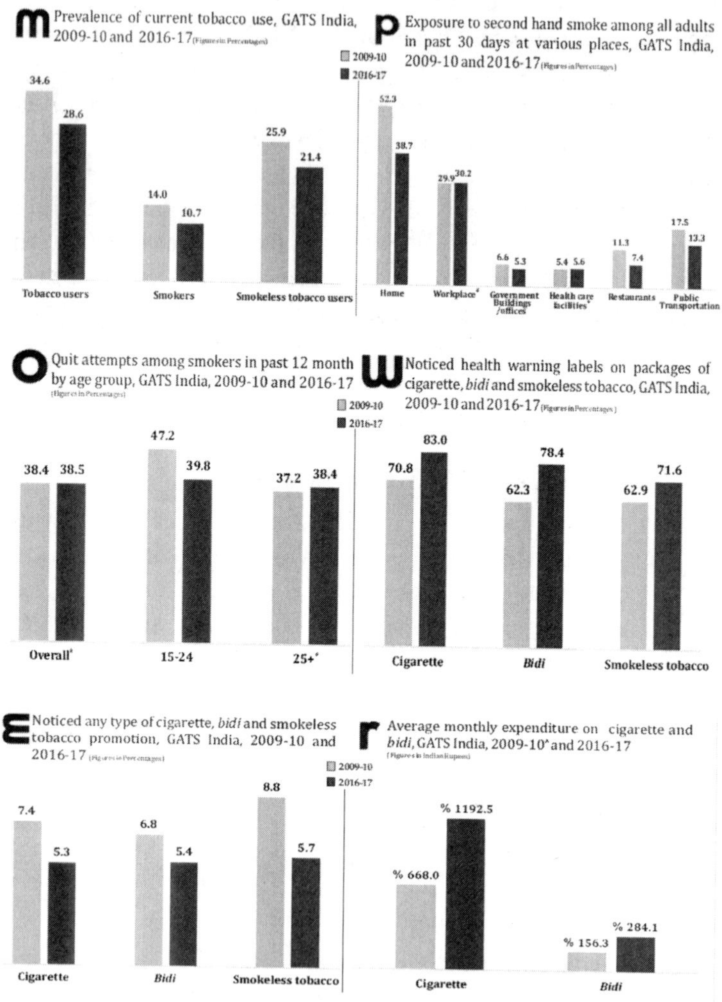

Source: Global Adult Tobacco Survey Fact Sheet India 2016-17 (WHO, 2018b).

A long-term study by Mishra et al. (2016) analyzed trends in smoking prevalence using data from the Special Fertility and Mortality Survey (1998), the Sample Registration System Baseline Survey (2004), and GATS (2010). Major findings include:

- Age-standardized smoking prevalence among men (15–69 years) declined modestly from 27% in 1998 to 24% in 2010, though it increased among those aged 15–29.
- Cigarette smoking more than doubled among men (15–69 years), and quadrupled in the 15–29 age group, while bidi smoking saw a slight decline.
- Women's smoking prevalence (15–69 years) was 2.7% in 2010, with about 11 million smokers in 2015.
- Smoking increased among illiterate men but decreased among those with 10 or more years of education.
- Ex-smoker rates among men aged 45–59 rose modestly but remained low.

The researchers warned of a shift from bidi to cigarette smoking—especially among young, less-educated men—and advocated for adaptive policy interventions, especially through taxation and pricing strategies.

Mohan and Lando (2016) catalogued the wide variety of smokeless tobacco (SLT) products used in India, such as gutkha, khaini, pan with tobacco, mawa, mishri, tuibur (used in Mizoram), and others—highlighting regional diversity in use and composition.

In a comprehensive review, Mohan et al. (2018) explored the social, economic, and health burdens of tobacco use. They discussed the impact of socioeconomic status, education, marriage, marketing practices, and price on tobacco use. Despite legislative efforts in India to regulate tobacco, enforcement remains a challenge. The authors emphasized the need for stronger anti-tobacco campaigns, greater public awareness, and proactive involvement of healthcare professionals and workplaces in cessation support.

2.2 Tobacco Consumption in Northeast India

The northeastern region of India, comprising eight states—Arunachal Pradesh, Assam, Manipur, Meghalaya, Mizoram, Nagaland, Sikkim, and Tripura—accounts for nearly 8% of India's total landmass. The region is marked by distinctive geographical, cultural, and socio-economic characteristics. Importantly, it consistently reports the highest prevalence of tobacco use in India (Dutt, 2018).

The Global Adult Tobacco Surveys (GATS) conducted in 2009–2010 and 2016–2017 revealed that tobacco use in several northeastern states, including Manipur, Assam, and Tripura, had increased over time. Particularly concerning is the high percentage of young tobacco users in the region. Adults in the Northeast remain one of the most vulnerable population subgroups in the country (Singh & Ladusingh, 2014). As noted by Sulabha Parasuraman, GATS-2 Consultant and Faculty at the Tata Institute of Social Sciences, the widespread use of tobacco by minors may stem from cultural acceptance and the strong influence of adult role models (Times of India, 2017).

Key highlights from GATS findings and regional reports include:

1. Tripura reported the highest tobacco use in the country at 64.5%, rising from 55.9% in 2009–10—an increase of 8.6 percentage points (Dutt, 2018).
2. Manipur, Tripura, and Assam reported prevalence rates of 55.1%, 64.5%, and 48.2% respectively. Manipur saw a 1-point increase, while Assam recorded a significant rise of 8.9 percentage points (Dutt, 2018).
3. Tripura had the highest prevalence of smokeless tobacco use at 48.5%, whereas Mizoram reported the highest rate of smoking at 34.4% (Dutt, 2018).
4. Sikkim showed a dramatic improvement, reducing its overall tobacco use from 41.6% to 17.9%, falling below the national average (The Morung Express, 2017).
5. While Sikkim, Mizoram, and Meghalaya showed progress in reducing tobacco use, Arunachal Pradesh and Manipur saw minimal improvements (The Morung Express, 2017).
6. The 15–17 years age group in the Northeast reported significantly higher tobacco use than the national average of 4.4%. Mizoram led with 27% of its youth using tobacco,

though this reflected a decline from 35.4% in 2009–10. Sikkim impressively reduced youth tobacco use from 11.6% to 0% (Times of India, 2017).

7. Arunachal Pradesh recorded an increase in youth tobacco use, rising from 14.3% to 25.1%. Other states followed: Meghalaya (12.6%), Tripura (11.6%), Nagaland (11.3%), Assam (9.1%), and Manipur (9%) (Times of India, 2017).

Further, a study by Ladusingh et al. (2017) using DLHS-4 data (2012–13) involving 27,706 youths aged 15–24 from the Northeast revealed that youth living with tobacco-using mothers were 3.4 times, and with tobacco-using fathers were 1.14 times more likely to use tobacco themselves. The researchers emphasized the urgent need to extend the National Tobacco Control Programme (NTCP) to the community level through the active involvement of civil society organisations to enhance awareness and support cessation efforts.

2.3 Tobacco Use in Mizoram: A Literature Overview

There exists a limited but growing body of literature focusing specifically on tobacco consumption in Mizoram. While several studies address tobacco use in the state within broader examinations of India or the Northeast region, a few notable doctoral theses have explored the psycho-social dimensions and health implications of tobacco use in Mizoram in depth.

Lalfakzuali (2014), in her doctoral research, examined the relationship between gender and levels of tobacco dependence in relation to various psychological variables such as personality traits, perceived stress, coping mechanisms, anxiety, and depression. Her study involved smokers, smokeless tobacco users, and non-users. She assessed how these psychological factors varied with the degree of tobacco dependence and evaluated the independent and interaction effects of gender and dependency levels. The findings revealed that female users scored higher than males across several psychological variables, including extraversion, neuroticism, perceived stress, anxiety, and depression. Among all groups, high-dependent female smokers reported the highest scores, followed by high-dependent smokeless tobacco users, low-dependent users, and finally, non-users. The study also identified significant interaction effects between gender and level of tobacco dependence on psychological well-being.

Hatzaw (2014), in her doctoral thesis titled *"Psychological Aspects of Tobacco Use among Mizo Women"*, investigated usage patterns, psycho-social drivers, motivations, and health impacts of tobacco consumption among Mizo women. She concluded that tobacco use was not significantly associated with education, occupation, or income levels. Moreover, awareness of health risks did not necessarily translate into attempts to quit. Her research found that smokeless tobacco was more commonly used by urban women, while smoking was more prevalent among rural women. Hatzaw underscored the importance of public engagement and the involvement of civil society organisations—such as the Tobacco Society of Mizoram and the Mizoram State Tobacco Control Society—in curbing tobacco use. She proposed a multi-level social work intervention strategy to address the issue comprehensively.

Hatzaw (2015) also conducted a community-based survey in Aizawl district in 2012 involving 350 healthy Mizo women aged 13 to 45. The objective was to assess tribal women's perceptions regarding the health consequences of tobacco use. The majority of respondents acknowledged the harmful effects of tobacco, identifying links with respiratory ailments, oral and esophageal cancers, and dental problems.

Vanlalngilneii and Thamilarasan (2016) explored the role of gender in influencing both tobacco consumption and cancer prevalence in Mizoram. They observed a strong gender-based distinction in tobacco use patterns, with males predominantly using smoked forms and females consuming smokeless varieties. These usage patterns were mirrored in cancer incidence statistics—for example, lung cancer was more prevalent among men, likely due to higher rates of smoking.

Despite Mizoram's progress in certain public health areas—such as achieving low levels of underweight children under five (NFHS-4,

2015–16) and consistently ranking high in the NITI Aayog Health Index for small states—the state continues to face major public health challenges. One persistent issue is the so-called *"Aizawl Syndrome"* (Chakraborty, 2017), where advanced medical infrastructure is concentrated in the capital, Aizawl, leaving rural and remote areas underserved. In addition, Mizoram struggles with a high burden of non-communicable diseases such as cancer, along with high rates of HIV/AIDS, drug abuse, and alcohol addiction.

Cancer remains one of the most pressing health concerns in the state. Mizoram records the highest cancer incidence rate in India, with around 1,400 new cases and approximately 700 cancer-related deaths annually (Karmakar, 2018). According to the Department of Economics and Statistics, Government of Mizoram (n.d.), cancer was the second leading cause of death in 2006, accounting for over 600 fatalities. A study by Varshney (2015) noted that between 1994 and 1998, Mizoram reported 347 cancer cases per 100,000 males—significantly higher than rates in cities like Chennai (79.3), Delhi (74.5), and rural Maharashtra (36.7), as per ICMR data. The Population-Based Cancer Registry (PBCR) report (ICMR, 2016) stated that Mizoram averaged 1,552 new cancer cases annually. Tonsing et al. (2018) attributed the high cancer burden to genetic predispositions, lifestyle choices, and environmental factors, especially the extensive use of tobacco and alcohol. Ankathil (2010) emphasized the need for further research into genetic vulnerabilities to cancer in the Mizo population, particularly in relation to tobacco use.

The Global Adult Tobacco Survey (GATS) 2016–2017 found that Mizoram had the second-highest prevalence of tobacco use in India at 58.7%, more than double the national average of 28.6% (Khojol, 2018; The Morung Express, 2018; TISS & MoHFW, 2018). In GATS 2009–2010, Mizoram had topped the list with a 67% tobacco use rate. Tobacco consumption in Mizoram includes both smoked forms (e.g., cigarettes and *zial*, a local cigar) and smokeless forms (e.g., *tuibur*, *sahdah*, *khaini*, *gutkha*).

Key findings from GATS 2 (2016–2017) include:

1. **Overall Decline**: Tobacco use decreased from 67.2% (GATS 1) to 58.7% (GATS 2), a reduction of 8.5 percentage points.
2. **Type-specific Decline**: Smoking and smokeless tobacco use declined by 5.3% and 7.2%, respectively.
3. **Gender Distribution**: 54.1% of men and 14.3% of women reported smoking. In contrast, 21.3% of men and 46% of women used smokeless tobacco.
4. **Youth Prevalence**: Mizoram recorded the highest tobacco use among adolescents aged 15–17 years at 27%, though it had decreased from 35.4% in GATS 1.
5. **Form of Use**: 25.1% of adults used only smoked tobacco, 24.3% used only smokeless forms, and 9.2% used both.
6. **Overall Prevalence by Gender**: 64.9% of men and 52.4% of women used some form of tobacco.
7. **Age of Initiation**: The average age of initiation rose slightly from 17.4 to 17.8 years.
8. **Secondhand Smoke**: Exposure to secondhand smoke declined significantly—at home (from 96.5% to 84.1%), at workplaces (64.6% to 44.4%), and in public places (27.3% to 18.2%).
9. **Expenditure Trends**: Monthly spending on cigarettes decreased from ₹1,201.5 to ₹712.6, while bidi expenditure slightly increased from ₹189.8 to ₹256.1.
10. **Health Professional Intervention**: 51.8% of smokers and 37.5% of smokeless tobacco users received advice from healthcare providers to quit.
11. **Impact of Warning Labels**: Only 17.2% of smokers and 26% of smokeless tobacco users reported considering quitting due to health warnings on packaging.
12. **Most Common Products**: Cigarettes (29.1%) and oral smokeless tobacco (21.6%) were the most widely used products.

These findings underscore the persistent and complex nature of tobacco use in Mizoram. Despite some improvement in prevalence rates, the state's tobacco burden remains disproportionately high, particularly among women and youth. The interplay of cultural norms, gender roles, inadequate rural healthcare infrastructure, and limited cessation support necessitates focused research and multi-dimensional public health strategies tailored to Mizoram's unique socio-cultural context.

* * * *

The high prevalence of tobacco use in India's northeastern region—particularly in Mizoram—continues to be a major public health concern. Mizoram reports an alarmingly high percentage of active tobacco users and correspondingly elevated rates of cancer-related mortality. The widespread addiction to tobacco has had detrimental effects on both the physical health and social wellbeing of Mizo society. However, data from the Global Adult Tobacco Survey (GATS) 2016–2017 offer a glimmer of hope. Compared to the 2009–2010 GATS results, Mizoram has seen a decline in overall tobacco use prevalence—from 67.2% to 58.7%. In addition, exposure to secondhand smoke has significantly decreased, from 96.5% to 84.1% in homes and from 64.6% to 44.4% in workplaces (The Morung Express, November 27, 2017).

Although Mizoram is no longer ranked as the state with the highest tobacco use in India—as was the case in the 2010 GATS survey—it still holds the unfortunate position of having the second-highest prevalence of tobacco use nationally (TISS & MoHFW, 2018). Despite the dedicated efforts of organisations such as the Mizoram State Tobacco Control Society (MSTCS) and NGOs like the Indian Society on Tobacco and Health (Mizoram Chapter) (Hmar, 2018; Khojol, 2018), the overall impact has been limited, and significant improvements remain elusive.

To design more effective and sustainable tobacco control programmes in Mizoram, it is imperative to investigate the deeper, underlying causes and motivational factors that drive tobacco addiction in the region. Given the state's distinct lifestyle patterns, psychological characteristics, and socio-cultural and economic contexts, conventional social marketing and intervention strategies—successful in other parts of India—may not yield the same results in Mizoram. Therefore, a comprehensive, locally sensitive social marketing strategy must be developed, one that takes into account the unique attributes of Mizo society and is informed by empirical insights into the region's tobacco consumption behaviours.

* * * *

Chapter - 3

Behind Tobacco Consumption: Culture, Society and Consumer Decision-Making

Understanding the extent of tobacco consumption in Mizoram requires more than just quantifying its prevalence—it demands a deeper exploration into the underlying factors and motivations that drive this widespread behaviour. Tobacco use in the state is shaped by a complex interplay of biological, psychological, socio-cultural, and economic influences (Glanz & Bishop, 2010). Therefore, a systematic and interdisciplinary approach is essential to examine how these diverse factors contribute to the initiation, continuation, addiction, and potential cessation of tobacco use. In addition to historical and cultural contexts, insights from the academic field of consumer behaviour offer valuable theoretical frameworks for analyzing such consumption patterns. By integrating these perspectives, tobacco use in Mizoram can be understood not merely as a public health concern, but as a broader socio-cultural phenomenon deeply embedded in the lived experiences of individuals and communities.

3.1 The History and Culture of Tobacco Consumption in Mizoram

Mizoram, meaning "land of the hill people" (Stevenson, 2024), is a landlocked state in northeastern India that attained full statehood on February 20, 1987 (Lalramhluni, 2020). While the early history of the state remains somewhat obscure, the Mizo people are believed to have originated from a Mongoloid migration from China. Their ancestral roots are traced to Shinlung, near the Yalung River, from where they are thought to have migrated through the Shan State, Kabaw Valley, and Chin Hills, eventually settling in the present-day Mizoram region by the 16th century (Hindustan Times, October 13, 2003). Mizoram's historical development has been influenced by a complex interplay of socio-political and economic factors, often shaped by periods of unrest and resistance. Though the state is now widely recognised for its peaceful environment and communal harmony, it continues to face persistent social challenges. Among the most pressing issues are high rates of substance abuse, including drug addiction, alcoholism, and an alarmingly high prevalence of tobacco use.

Tobacco consumption has long been intertwined with cultural practices in many parts of India, and Mizoram is no exception. In several regions, tobacco use has historically been linked to social status and community rituals (Rath, 2010). For instance, in Kerala, tobacco was traditionally offered during significant celebrations such as marriages (Thankappan & Thresia, 2007). In Northeast India, the roots of tobacco consumption can be traced back to the tradition of opium smoking, which was banned in the 1960s (Transnational Institute, 2011). Similarly, tobacco use in Mizoram carries cultural significance, with gender roles playing a central part in shaping tobacco consumption patterns. Vanlalngilneii and Thamilarasan (2016) highlight how these roles dictate the types of tobacco products consumed by men and women.

The earliest evidence of smoking-related practices in Mizoram has been identified through excavations carried out by the Archaeological Survey of India (ASI) at Vangchhia in Champhai District—Mizoram's first officially protected archaeological site. Among the carvings on the menhirs are depictions of human figures with smoking pipes affixed to their mouths (Nayan & Singh, 2022), suggesting a symbolic or cultural association with smoking[1]. The

1. While the menhirs at Vangchhia depict human figures with pipe-like objects held to their mouths, it would be anachronistic to conclude these represent tobacco smoking. Tobacco is native to the Americas and was introduced

exact age of these menhirs is yet to be conclusively determined. However, based on radiocarbon dating conducted by two different agencies, they can be broadly placed within a period spanning about nine centuries — from the 7th to the 15th century AD. (Nayan, 2018). However, given the likely chronological gap between the early settlers of the present-day Mizo population and the ancient inhabitants of the Vangchhia region, any suggestion of specific cultural exchange remains speculative and cannot be conclusively established.

Exhibit 3.1: Carved Human Figure with Smoking Pipe on a Vangchhia Menhir

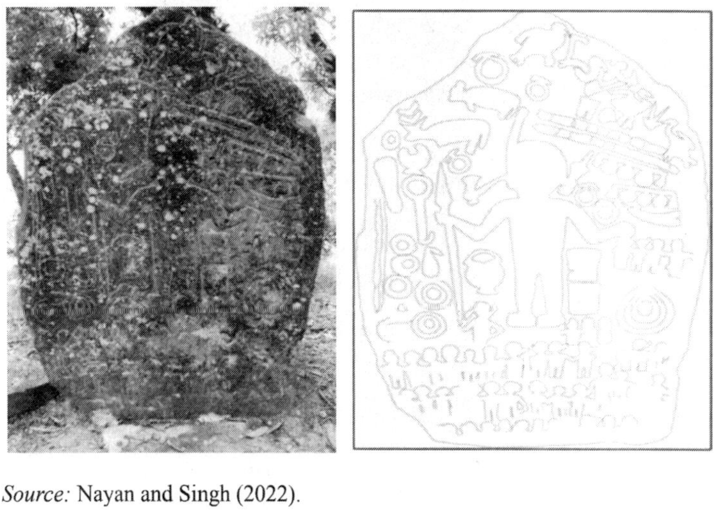

Source: Nayan and Singh (2022).

Mizoram also has a rich tradition of consuming *Kuhva*, a combination of betel leaf, areca nut, and slaked lime, which, though not containing tobacco, is highly addictive. Areca nut, considered the fourth most widely used psychoactive substance globally (after

to the Indian subcontinent and South Asia only around 16th century, whereas the Vangchhia menhirs, though yet to be conclusively dated, may predate this period by a significant margin. It is more likely that the depicted objects may instead have symbolic or ceremonial meanings, or could represent other forms of indigenous smoking practices involving different herbs or plant materials.

caffeine, alcohol, and nicotine), adds a complex layer to tobacco-related health concerns (Gupta & Ray, 2004a). The age-old tradition of offering betel leaf, areca nut, and slaked lime as a gesture of warm hospitality is deeply rooted in the socio-cultural practices of many communities across Northeast India (Ahuja & Ahuja, 2011).

Historically, tobacco use in Mizoram was connected to agricultural practices, particularly as a tool to repel insects and mosquitoes while working in the fields. Women, during the early stages of pregnancy, also used tobacco in the form of *Zial*[1] ashes to relieve nausea and discomfort, and tobacco leaves were kept at home as a first aid disinfectant (Hatzaw, 2014). In traditional Mizo society, tobacco consumption was so culturally embedded that even its use by children, irrespective of gender drew little objection or concern (Shakespear, 1975). The primary forms of tobacco consumed by the

Exhibit 3.2: Traditional Smoking and Tobacco Consumption Tools Used in Mizoram

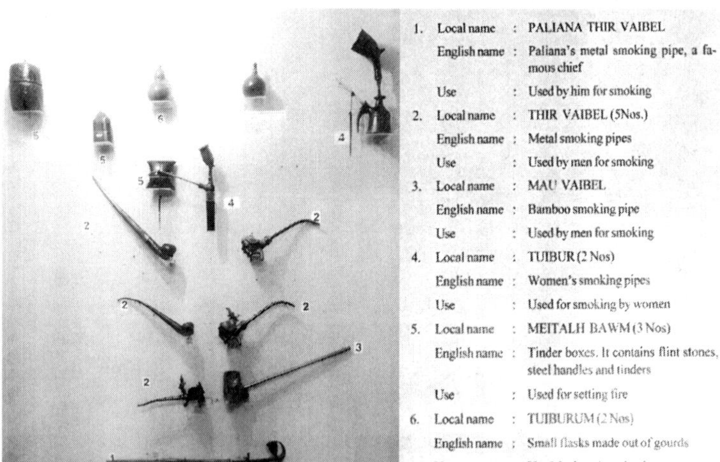

Source: Public Display at Mizoram State Museum, Aizawl.

1. Zial or Zozial is a locally made rolled tobacco used for smoking in Mizoram.

Mizos include smoking nicotine rolls (*Vaihlozial/Zozial*), using water pipes (*Vaibel*), and consuming tobacco-infused water orally (*Tuibur*) (Hatzaw, 2014). Exhibit 3.2 shows the various traditional smoking and tobacco consumption tools used in Mizoram.

Vanhnuailiana (1800–1871), the chief of the Eastern Lushai Hills, possessed a highly valued cultural artifact known as *Tuburum Phir*—a pair of twin gourds traditionally used to contain nicotine-infused water. This object held significant symbolic and social value, and its use was restricted to a select circle; Vanhnuailiana shared it only with his closest confidants, never with ordinary members of the community (Tribal Research Institute, 1993).

The reference of tobacco in Mizo folklore, art, and music also reflects its deep-rooted cultural importance. For instance, pipe smoking was an old and widespread practice among the Mizos, with numerous candid references found in their folklore. One such example appears in the following excerpt from a folktale titled *Mualzavata* (Pachuau, 2008):

> "One day Mualzavata was smoking a pipe. He placed his pipe in the narrow pass between two hills and some of his friends saw him doing so and they decided to play a practical joke on him. Soon they stuffed the pipe with bamboo and several other pieces of wood that were waiting to be burnt for jhum cultivation. Mualzavata was oblivious to the prank and so he picked up his pipe and puffed away at it with a vehemence. The skies began to darken every time he puffed away and the people became alarmed and cried, "Hey... it is about to rain.""

Historical artworks, such as R. G. Woodthorpe's 1872 watercolour paintings (Exhibit 3.3), depict portraits of Lushai men and women proudly holding traditional smoking pipes (Pachuau & Schendel, 2015). Beyond being a part of everyday life, these depictions may also suggest that pipe smoking among the Mizos was associated with social status and served as an expression of individual sophistication. The arrival of foreign tobacco products such as cigarettes and cigars during the colonial period further entrenched tobacco use in Mizoram, making it even more prevalent especially among the affluent.

Exhibit 3.3: 1872 Portraits of Lushai Men and Women with Traditional Smoking Pipes

Watercolours by R. G. Woodthorpe (1872)

Women in traditional Mizo society were expected to be proficient in preparing *Zozial*, a practice that was also celebrated in Mizo music. A popular song by Pu Vankhama (1930) glorifies the habit of smoking Mizo tobacco, emphasizing its local origins and unique flavor (Chawngthanmawii, 2014). The song illustrates how tobacco was associated with cultural pride and social bonding.

"Mizo Vailhlo hi zuk ching la
(Cultivate the habit of smoking Mizo tobacco),
Tuiber mai, Aw Sangau, Zurpui leh Kauzing
(The sweetest being Sangau, Zurpui and hauzing brand):
Sen a tlem a hriselna Zoram thil ani bawk
(It is economical, harmless, and besides it is Zoram origin),
Tui ber ah chuan lengi zial tr ang che
(But for the sweetest flavour, ask your fiancé to roll it)"

The practice of tobacco consumption, particularly cigarette smoking, was further reinforced among the youth and integrated into Mizo culture through the rise of television and movies in the latter half of the 20th century. As a result, smoking gradually became a defining element of popular culture in Mizoram. Tobacco use evolved into a symbol of friendship and generosity among the youth, as it increasingly represented an integral part of Mizo lifestyle and commensality (Vanlalngilneii & Thamilarasan, 2016). In this way, tobacco consumption in Mizoram became not just a habit, but a significant cultural expression deeply embedded in both social life and identity.

In addition to the widespread availability of Indian tobacco products, the contemporary markets in Mizoram are also flooded with cheap, contraband tobacco products, particularly cigarettes originating from China and Myanmar. The affordability of these products has made tobacco consumption more accessible to a larger segment of the population. Despite the recent decline in tobacco prevalence, from a concerning 67.2% to 58.7%, thanks to stricter enforcement of the Cigarettes and Other Tobacco Products Act (COTPA) and the proactive efforts of the Mizoram State Tobacco Control Society (MSTCS) (Health & Family Welfare Department, Government of Mizoram, 2018), a tobacco use rate of 58.7% remains alarmingly high for any society.

3.2 Socioeconomic and Familial Influences on Tobacco Use

Mizoram is one of the fastest-growing smaller states in India, with a growth rate of 7.9% and an economy valued at ₹14,400 crore in the financial year 2021 (Tyagi, 2022). According to the 2011 Census, Mizoram had a total population of 10,97,206, a sex ratio of 976, and a low population density of only 52 persons per square kilometer (PPID, 2023). Notably, Mizoram is among the most urbanised states in the region. As per the 2011 Census, 51.5% of its population resides in urban areas—significantly higher than the combined urban population of all Northeastern states (18.3%) and the national average (31.2%) (Directorate of Economics & Statistics [DES], 2018). Aizawl, the state capital and largest city, has a population of 4,00,309 (DES, 2018).

Mizoram was officially declared as the first fully literate state in India on May 20, 2025, with a literacy rate of 98.20% as per the 2023–24 PFLS survey (PIB, 2025). In terms of health indicators, Mizoram recorded a 10% drop, in Infant Mortality Rate in 2019–20, reaching 5 per 1,000 live births—second only to Nagaland (The New Indian Express, May 10, 2020). In the *India Happiness Report 2020*, Mizoram was ranked as the happiest state in India (Times of India, September 22, 2020). According to the Economic Survey 2017–18 by the Ministry of Finance, Government of India, the per capita income of Mizoram in 2015–16 was ₹1,14,524—substantially higher than that of the Northeastern states combined (₹1,01,631.60) and the national average (₹94,130) (PPID, 2018). The state's projected per capita income for 2021–22 has further increased to ₹1,75,896 (PPID, 2023).

At prevailing market prices, Mizoram's Gross State Domestic Product (GSDP) for 2024–25 is provisionally estimated at ₹48,038 crore (US$ 5.77 billion) (IBEF, 2024). Agriculture remains the backbone of Mizoram's economy, with approximately 70% of the population engaged in some form of agricultural activity. Forests cover about 85.41% of the state's geographical area, including around 3,267 square kilometers of bamboo forest (India Brand Equity Foundation [IBEF], 2023). The state has a bamboo stock of 25.26 million metric tonnes across 35 different varieties (IBEF, 2023). Sericulture is another key industry in Mizoram. In 2018–19, raw silk production reached 75 metric tonnes (IBEF, 2019). Additionally, sectors such as food and agro-processing, hydro power, tourism, handloom, and horticulture have been identified as having significant potential for economic development. Mizoram also enjoys a strategic geographical location, sharing domestic borders with Manipur, Tripura, and Assam, and international borders with Bangladesh and Myanmar—providing unique opportunities for cross-border trade and cooperation.

The term "socioeconomic" refers to a field of study that examines how social and economic factors interact to influence various aspects of life (Business Dictionary, 2019). Socioeconomic status is typically measured through indicators such as education, income, and occupation (Baker, 2014). According to Barik et al. (2016), selecting the most appropriate indicators of socioeconomic position is crucial to gaining a comprehensive understanding of social inequities in tobacco use. Reddy and Gupta (2004) emphasized the need for researchers to identify the economic and socio-cultural determinants of tobacco use across different demographic groups in India. Similarly, Reddy et al. (2010) identified the economic impact of tobacco use, as well as the social determinants of tobacco consumption, as top research priorities for tobacco control in low- and middle-income countries.

Mathur et al. (2014) highlighted that socioeconomic disparities in tobacco use during adolescence often serve as a precursor to broader inequalities in tobacco-related health outcomes in adulthood. Numerous studies have consistently shown that factors such as income, education, caste, gender, age, and region of residence are significantly associated with tobacco use (Ahmed & Peeran, 2016; Fouad et al., 2016; Lal et al., 2015; Mini et al., 2014; Rawat et al., 2015; Singh & Ladusingh, 2014; Thakur et al., 2015; Thankappan & Thresia, 2007; Turk et al., 2012), and are strong predictors of smoking behaviour (Yaya et al., 2017). Gordon et al. (2004) found robust, independent effects of socioeconomic status and social class on health behaviours such as smoking, alcohol consumption, and tobacco chewing. Moreover, tobacco use not only contributes to poverty (John, 2005), but also perpetuates a vicious cycle of social problems, impeding the development of individuals, households, and nations (Eriksen et al., 2012; Eriksen et al., 2015). As a result, tobacco control is increasingly recognised as a vital strategy for promoting economic development and reducing poverty, especially in low- and middle-income countries (Novotny & Mamudu, 2008).

The period of adolescence and early adulthood has been consistently identified as the most vulnerable time for the initiation of tobacco use in India (Jindal et al., 2005; National Sample Survey Organisation [NSSO], 1998; Reddy & Gupta, 2004). In Mizoram, the average age of initiation for any form of tobacco use is 17.8 years, with 17.5 years for smoking and 18.3 years for smokeless tobacco (TISS &

MHFW, 2018). This age range closely aligns with the college-going population, making undergraduate students a critical demographic for studying tobacco consumption behaviour. Moreover, college students, in general, operate within a less restrictive environment compared to school students, often enjoying increased autonomy and exposure to social settings where behaviours such as smoking and drinking are more accessible and socially accepted (Maggs, 1997; O'Malley & Johnston, 2002). Considering this, my doctoral research focused on examining the relationship between select socio-economic factors and tobacco consumption among undergraduate students in Mizoram. Primary data was collected from a randomly selected sample of 500 students from Pachhunga University College in Aizawl district and Government Saiha College in Siaha district. Respondents were categorised into three groups based on their tobacco usage at the time of the survey: Active Tobacco Consumers (ATC), Past Tobacco Consumers (PTC), and Non-Tobacco Consumers (NTC)[1]. Out of the total respondents, 63.2% were Active Tobacco Consumers, 28.6% were Non-Tobacco Consumers, and 8.2% were Past Tobacco Consumers.

The important findings about the socio-economic profile of ATC are as follows:

- Majority of the active tobacco consumers (63.6%) consumes tobacco daily followed by 19.9% of them who consumes it occasionally (once in a week), followed by 16.5% of them who consumes it 3 to 4 days a week.

---

1. A simplified categorisation of tobacco users has been devised which combines both Smokers and Smokeless Tobacco Users and categorizes them under three basic categories as follows:
   (i) Active Tobacco Consumers (ATC): It includes Daily Smokers, Daily Users, Occasional Smokers and Occasional Users and is similar to the definition of current tobacco use by Fouad et al., (2016).
   (ii) Past Tobacco Consumers (PTC): It includes Ex-Smokers and Ex-Users as per WHO (1983) categorisation of tobacco users.
   (iii) Non Tobacco Consumers (NTC): It includes Non-Smokers, Non-Users, Other Smokers and Other Users as per WHO (1983) categorisation of tobacco users.

- 88.6% of all ATC were aged between 18 to 23 years. The average age of the ATC was 20.71 years.
- Gender wise, 54.1% of the ATC were males and 45.9% of the ATC were females.
- 65.19% of the ATC were having 4 to 6 members in their families, followed by 23.42% of them who have 7 to 10 members in their families and only 6.33% of them having 4 or less members in their families.
- In terms of relationship status[1], 75.3% of the ATC were single, 9.2% of them confessed to be in an open relationship whereas 7.6% of them were in a committed relationship.
- More than half (51.27%) of the ATC's average monthly household income is somewhere between ₹10,000 to ₹30,000.
- 44.6% of the ATC's primary family occupation is service followed by business (28.2%), followed by farming (20.3%).
- Most of the ATC (80.1%) in Mizoram spends ₹30 or less for consuming tobacco on a daily basis.
- 59.5% of the ATC are found to be financially dependent, followed by 22.2% who are partially financially dependent on their families and only 18.4% of them are financially independent.
- 40.5% of the ATC either strongly agrees or agrees that they have tobacco related health problems. However, 39.9% of them are also not sure that they have any health problems that are caused due to tobacco consumption.
- Majority of the ATC (83.5%) have members in the family who consumes tobacco.

1. The respondents were asked to reveal their relationship status under few predefined categories namely, "Single" (having no partner), "In an open relationship" (having one or more partner without any commitment), "In a committed relationship" (having commitment with a single partner), "In a complicated relationship" (having one or more partner where the nature of relationship is taboo or difficult to define), "Married" and "Divorced.

- Spending time with families, friends and surfing the internet are some of the most popular activities performed by the ATC.
- The average age of initiation of tobacco by ATC is 15.89 years.

The important findings from the comparison of socio-economic profiles between ATC, NTC and PTC are as follows:

- The average age of the ATC (20.71 years) was slightly higher compared to the PTC (20.24 years) and NTC (20.2 years) among the respondents.
- 54.11% ATC among the respondents were males and 45.89% were females. 62.24% NTC among the respondents were females and 37.76% were males. Therefore, tobacco consumption is more prevalent among male undergraduate students than female undergraduate students among the respondents.
- The percentage of PTC who belongs to medium sized families of 4 to 6 members is comparatively higher (80.49%) than the percentage of NTC (62.94%) and ATC (65.19%) who belongs to similar sized families.
- In terms of relationship status of the respondents, most of them were single and the percentage of singles is highest (83.22%) among the NTC. However, the percentage of undergraduate students who were in an open relationship is highest (9.18%) among the ATC and the percentage of undergraduate students who were in a complicated relationship is highest (7.32%) among the PTC.
- The PTC among the respondents have the highest percentage of students who have less than ₹10,000 as their average monthly family income and also, they have less percentage of students having monthly household income of ₹10,001 to ₹20,000, ₹20,001 to ₹30,000 and more than ₹40,000 compared to NTC and ATC. Therefore, could the economic constraints be a key factor for the motivation to quit tobacco

among the PTC? And could higher income or affordability be another key factor for many undergraduate ATC to continue the habit of tobacco consumption?

- Service is the most common family occupation across respondents. However, business is the second most common family occupation only for ATC whereas farming is the second most common primary family occupation for both NTC and PTC. Also, there are very less respondents whose family's primary occupation includes pension and other sources but PTC includes slightly higher (9.76%) percentage of students whose family's primary occupation involves pension.
- 80.06% of the ATC and 92.68% of the PTC among the respondents used to spend ₹30 or less daily on tobacco consumption. 70.73% of the PTC among the respondents used to spend less than ₹10 daily on tobacco.
- The percentage of financially dependent students is more among NTC (68.53%) than ATC (59.49%) and PTC (58.54%) among the respondents. Whereas, financially independent students are also more among both ATC (18.35%) and PTC (19.51%) compared to NTC (17.48%) among the respondents. This might indicate that, students who are financially independent or partially dependent are more inclined towards tobacco consumption than students who are financially dependent.
- Most of the ATC and PTC among the respondents agree that they have health problems caused due to their habit of consuming tobacco. However, the percentage of PTC (26.83%) is slightly more compared to ATC (19.62%) who either strongly disagrees or disagrees that they have tobacco related health problems.
- There are more ATC (83.54%) than NTC (72.73%) and PTC (80.49%) among the respondents who have members in the family who consumes tobacco. Therefore, tobacco

consumption by family members seems to have an influence on students who consumes or consumed tobacco in the past.

- Most of the respondents spend considerable amount of time with their families and friends and moderate amount of time in watching television daily. Listening to music is popular among most respondents and majority of the respondents spends lengthy hours daily in surfing the internet.
- The average age of initiation to tobacco for the total 357 tobacco consumers (ATC and PTC) is 15.64 years, 15.89 years for ATC and 13.73 years for PTC. Due to such early age of initiation to tobacco among the students, it may be necessary to start educating students regarding the harmful effects of tobacco in schools and strictly control tobacco consumption at the school level.

A Percentage-wise comparison along with Pearson Chi-Square Test and Fisher's Exact Test were also carried out to test the level of significant association between socio-economic factors and tobacco user categories. The socio-economic factors selected for comparison includes family size, relationship status, family income, family occupation, financial dependency and tobacco consumption in the family. The findings from the comparative analysis between ATC, PTC and NTC are as follows:

(a) **Comparison of Family Size:** A test of significance shows that there is no significant association between family size and tobacco user categories as the p value (Fisher's exact test) is 0.316 (i.e., $p>.05$). Therefore, family sizes are not determining factor for consumption of tobacco by undergraduate tobacco consumers in Mizoram.

(b) **Comparison of Relationship Status:** The Pearson Chi-Square Test shows significant level of 0.753 (i.e., $p>0.05$), indicating a non-significant association between tobacco user category and their relationship status. Therefore, it is evident that the relationship status of the undergraduate students is not a determining factor for their choice of tobacco consumption.

(c) **Comparison of Family Income:** A Pearson Chi-Square test reveals that there is no significant association between family income and tobacco user category as the p value is 0.223 (i.e., $p>.05$).

(d) **Comparison of Family Occupation:** The Fisher's Exact Test shows significant level of 0.251 (i.e., $p>0.05$), indicating a non-significant association between tobacco user category and family occupation. Therefore, family occupation may not be regarded as a determining factor for tobacco consumption among undergraduate students in Mizoram.

(e) **Comparison of Financial Dependency:** There may be a slight tendency among the respondents who are less financially dependent on their families to feel free to buy and consume tobacco products. However, the Pearson Chi-Square Test shows significant level of 0.300 (i.e., $p>0.05$), indicating a non-significant association between tobacco user category and their status of financial dependency.

(f) **Comparison of Tobacco Consumption in Family:** The tobacco consumption in the family members of both ATC and PTC are comparatively higher than the tobacco consumption in the family members of NTC. The Fisher's exact test also indicates a significant (0.042) p value (i.e., $p<0.05$), therefore, there is a significant association between tobacco consumption in family and tobacco user category. So, it may be concluded that tobacco consumption in the family does have an influence on undergraduate student's choice of tobacco consumption.

While prior studies have consistently demonstrated a strong link between various socio-economic factors and tobacco consumption, the present study reveals a contrasting outcome. It was found that there is no statistically significant association between a respondent's tobacco consumption status and socio-economic variables such as family size, relationship status, family income, family occupation, and financial dependency. Therefore, these factors do not appear to be determining influences on tobacco use among undergraduate students in Mizoram.

However, a significant association was observed between tobacco consumption within the respondent's family and their own tobacco use. This suggests that exposure to tobacco use by family members may influence individuals—especially young adults—to adopt similar habits. In this context, the family emerges as a crucial support system, particularly during the vulnerable transition from adolescence to adulthood. This finding underscores the need to raise awareness among families in Mizoram about the impact of their own tobacco use on the younger generation. Promoting responsible behaviour and preventive measures within the household is essential for safeguarding the health and wellbeing of youth and curbing the intergenerational transmission of tobacco habits.

3.3 Tobacco Use through the Lens of Consumer Decision-Making

Understanding the underlying factors and motivations behind the widespread tobacco consumption in Mizoram is crucial. An explorative study of tobacco consumption behaviour is thus warranted to examine the social, psychological, economic, and cultural influences that contribute to initiation, addiction, and cessation. Loudon and Bitta (2002) emphasize that "understanding consumer (consumption) behaviour from a macro perspective can provide insight into aggregate economic and social trends and can perhaps even predict such trends. In addition, this understanding may suggest ways to increase the efficiency of the market system and improve the well-being of people in society." Central to this understanding is the consumer decision-making process, which plays a critical role in shaping consumption behaviour. In the case of tobacco, this process is particularly significant, as it involves injurious consumption—behaviour that negatively impacts long-term health and well-being (Hawkins et al., 2010).

Tobacco consumption decisions are influenced by a complex interplay of factors that vary across regions and communities.

Therefore, organisations and agencies engaged in tobacco control—especially those employing social marketing strategies—must integrate localised knowledge of consumer behaviour and decision-making to enhance the effectiveness of their interventions. In this context, the guiding research question— *"What is the decision-making process adopted for consuming tobacco products by undergraduate tobacco consumers in Mizoram?"*—frames the inquiry. To address this, both primary and secondary data were utilised. The primary data was collected from a sample of 500 undergraduate students across two selected colleges in Mizoram, offering critical insights into the patterns and processes underlying tobacco consumption in this demographic.

Consumer behaviour is broadly defined as "the decision process and physical activity individuals engage in when evaluating, acquiring, using, or disposing of goods and services" (Loudon & Bitta, 2002). Hawkins et al. (2007, p. 6) further expand this definition, describing it as "the study of individuals, groups, or organisations and the processes they use to select, secure, use, and dispose of products, services, experiences, or ideas to satisfy needs, and the impacts that these processes have on the consumer and society."

According to the World Health Organisation (WHO, n.d.), tobacco consumption is influenced by various factors, including product price, consumer income, demographic and socioeconomic characteristics, area of residence (urban or rural), tobacco control interventions, and awareness about the health effects of tobacco use. Additionally, previous studies have linked tobacco use to psychological and personality traits such as extraversion (Eysenck et al., 1960; Lalfakzuali, 2014), neuroticism (Choi et al., 2017; Kulkarni et al., 2018; Lalfakzuali, 2014), conscientiousness (Choi et al., 2017), and risk-taking behaviour (Lejuez et al., 2003; 2005; Ristache & Rotărescu, 2015). In her doctoral research, Lalfakzuali (2014) examined the relationship between gender and levels of tobacco dependence in Mizoram, focusing on psychological variables such as personality, stress, coping mechanisms, anxiety, and depression among smokers, smokeless tobacco users, and non-users.

To understand tobacco consumption among undergraduate students in Mizoram, it is essential to logically explain the decision-making process using appropriate consumer behaviour models. All relevant factors specific to the Mizoram context must be explored to contextualise the consumption behaviour and decision-making pathway. One widely accepted framework is the traditional "five-stage model" of consumer decision-making, which comprises five key steps: need recognition, information search, evaluation of alternatives, purchase decision, and post-purchase behaviour (Kotler & Keller, 2012; Stankevich, 2017). Another influential model is proposed by Schiffman and Kanuk (2007), which simplifies the consumer decision-making process into three interrelated stages:

- **(a) Input:** This stage examines external influences that stimulate the desire to consume, such as marketing activities and sociocultural factors.
- **(b) Process:** This stage involves the internal psychological mechanisms of decision-making, including need recognition, information search, evaluation of alternatives, and personal experiences.
- **(c) Output:** This final stage focuses on the actual purchase decision and the post-purchase evaluation.

This model is conceptually aligned with the earlier Engel, Kollat, and Blackwell (1968) model, which also incorporates input, information processing, decision-making components, and influencing variables.

Another influential model in social psychology and consumer decision-making is the Theory of Reasoned Action (TRA), one of the most widely applied frameworks for understanding behavioural intentions (Donovan & Henley, 2010). Developed by Fishbein and Ajzen (1975), the theory suggests that a specific behaviour is primarily determined by an individual's intention to perform that behaviour. These intentions, in turn, are shaped by two key factors: attitude toward the behaviour and subjective norm. An individual's attitude toward a behaviour is based on their beliefs about the outcomes or consequences of performing the behaviour, each weighted by their evaluation of those consequences. For instance, if someone believes that smoking tobacco will help reduce stress (a perceived benefit), and they value stress relief highly, this will strengthen a positive attitude toward smoking. The subjective norm, on the other hand, refers to an individual's perception of social pressure—that is, the beliefs about whether significant others (such as peers, family, or society at large) think they should or should not perform the behaviour. This is further moderated by the individual's motivation to comply with those perceived expectations.

Exhibit 3.4: A Model of Consumer Decision Making

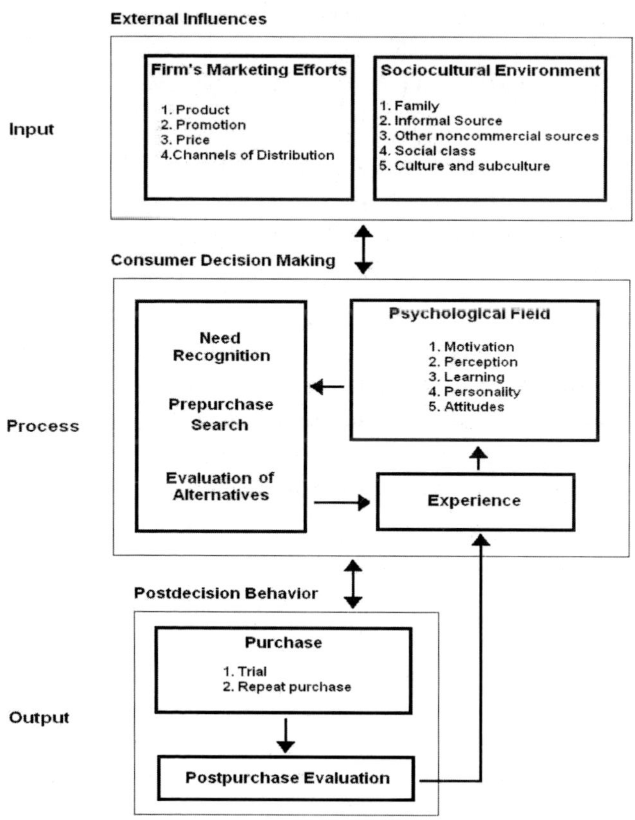

Source: Schiffman and Kanuk (2007) p. 36.

In the context of tobacco consumption, the TRA can be a valuable tool for understanding how individuals form intentions based on their own attitudes toward smoking and their perceptions of social expectations. It sheds light on how people assess the personal and social consequences of tobacco use (whether positive, negative, or neutral), and the degree to which they are influenced by others' behaviours or norms in their community. Thus, the TRA provides a structured framework to predict and explain tobacco consumption intentions and behaviours, particularly among populations such as undergraduate students, where peer influence and social conformity may play significant roles. Therefore, applying both these models allows for a structured and comprehensive understanding of how undergraduate consumers in Mizoram arrive at decisions regarding tobacco use, and offers valuable insights for interventions targeting behaviour change.

Based on Schiffman and Kanuk's (2007) model of consumer decision-making (Exhibit 3.4), the decision-making process for tobacco consumption adopted by the undergraduate students in the select colleges of Mizoram may be explained as follows:

(A) **The Input Stage:** According to the primary data, during the input stage of tobacco consumption behaviour, undergraduate respondents are subjected to two major sources of external influence. Firstly, they are exposed to the marketing efforts of tobacco companies and sellers; secondly, they are influenced by their socio-cultural environment.

Due to stringent legal restrictions, tobacco marketing in Mizoram relies heavily on passive and subliminal strategies such as point-of-sale displays, attractive packaging, widespread and targeted distribution, and indirect promotion through media platforms like films, the internet, and social media. Key factors that motivate tobacco consumption include the sight of tobacco products on shop displays, portrayals of tobacco use in movies or television, and indirect advertisements related to tobacco. Survey findings reveal that 28% of respondents agreed that attractive packaging increases their desire to smoke or consume tobacco, while 40.4% disagreed and 31.6% were uncertain. Notably, 89.8% of respondents acknowledged that tobacco products are available within 100 yards of their campuses—highlighting the strategic and pervasive distribution efforts by tobacco companies to target the younger demographic.

Socio-cultural influences also play a critical role. Family emerges as an important factor, with a majority (65.8%) of respondents belonging to families with 4 to 6 members. Their families are primarily engaged in service, business, or farming, and 69.8% have an average monthly household income of ₹30,000 or below. While 62% of the respondents are financially dependent on their families, the proportion is higher among NTC (68.53%) compared to ATC (59.49%) and PTC (58.54%). A significant 80.2% of respondents reported that one or more family members consume tobacco. This prevalence is higher among ATC (83.54%) than NTC (72.73%), and there is a statistically significant association between family tobacco consumption and the respondent's tobacco user category. This suggests a direct or indirect familial influence in the initiation or reinforcement of the habit.

When asked about who influenced them directly, most ATC and PTC respondents identified 'friends' as the key initiators. Additionally, 17.2% of respondents admitted that they find it unfriendly to refuse tobacco when offered by others, indicating strong peer pressure as a major factor. Besides friends, other social influences include 'common people in the society', 'relatives', and 'siblings'. Generally, contemporary Mizo society does not express strong disapproval toward tobacco use. Only 52% of respondents reported that they object to their partner's smoking or tobacco habits; the rest were either indifferent or uncertain. A notable 16.46% of ATC respondents, compared to only 3.5% of NTC, consider smoking fashionable. Moreover, 31.8% of all respondents view tobacco consumption as a convenient way to socialise.

These perceptions are significantly associated with the tobacco user category.

Despite a degree of social acceptance, a large majority of respondents are aware of the health risks associated with tobacco. Approximately 86% agree that tobacco use increases the risk of cancer, and 89% acknowledge that smoking or tobacco consumption can be fatal. This reveals a dissonance between awareness and behaviour—many undergraduate students continue to consume tobacco despite understanding its harmful effects.

(B) The Process Stage: This stage involves the actual decision-making process of the consumer regarding tobacco consumption. Various psychological factors—such as motivation, perception, learning, personality, and attitudes—interact with external influences from the input stage to shape how a consumer recognizes a need, searches for information, and evaluates alternatives. These internal psychological mechanisms influence, and are simultaneously influenced by, the consumer's environment (Schiffman & Kanuk, 2007).

Among undergraduate tobacco consumers, the most commonly reported consumption motivator is '*the conscious thought of personal possession of tobacco products*'. This is closely followed by '*the physical sight of others consuming or smoking tobacco*'. Other frequently cited influences include '*the display of tobacco products in shops, portrayals of tobacco use in movies or television*, and *exposure to tobacco-related advertisements*'. These stimuli reinforce the motivation to consume tobacco. Furthermore, 28% of all respondents—including 29.11% of the ATC and 36.59% of the PTC—agreed that the attractive design and branding of tobacco products increases their desire to consume them. The influence of packaging appears to extend beyond conscious perception, potentially operating at a subliminal level to enhance consumer appeal.

During a word association exercise, more than half of the respondents (51%) associated the word *tobacco* with '*Addictive*', followed by 31.6% who associated it with '*Harmful*'. Notably, 60.76% of ATC respondents considered tobacco '*Addictive*', whereas 48.95% of NTC respondents described it as '*Harmful*'. Additionally, 11.39% of the ATC linked the term '*Pleasurable*' with tobacco, while 13.99% of the NTC associated it with '*Annoying*'. This indicates a subtle perceptual divide between ATC and NTC respondents and suggests different cognitive and emotional responses to tobacco consumption. Regarding the cost perception, a significant proportion (68.6%) of respondents considered tobacco consumption to be expensive. This perception also showed a significant association with tobacco user category, highlighting how economic considerations intersect with psychological and behavioural factors.

The personality traits and attitudes of undergraduate tobacco users play a pivotal role in their decision-making. There is a strong correlation between tobacco consumption and other addictive behaviours such as alcohol and drug use, suggesting a broader pattern of risk-taking or addictive tendencies among these students. Among the ATC respondents, 57.91% agreed that tobacco consumption is a personal choice and should not be subjected to external judgment, while 51.75% of NTC respondents disagreed with this view—reflecting a stronger pro-tobacco attitude among active users. Further, 14.56% of ATC respondents agreed that tobacco consumption makes them appear 'cool and mature' in front of others, compared to only 4.9% of NTC respondents having similar views. This illustrates how social image and identity also influence consumption behaviour.

Collectively, these psychological factors—motivation, perception, learning, personality, and attitudes—shape the consumer's need recognition, pre-purchase search, and evaluation of alternatives. While evaluating the various alternatives, the undergraduate tobacco consumers mostly consider factors such as 'easy availability', 'flavour and feel' and 'low price'. The experiences from this evaluation further strengthens the psychological field consisting motivation, perception, learning, personality and attitude which again affects the stages of need recognition, pre-purchase search and evaluation of alternatives for tobacco consumption by undergraduate tobacco consumers. Thus, these evaluative experiences reinforce their psychological orientations, creating a feedback loop that continually influences future stages of consumption decision-making.

(C) **The Output Stage:** The output stage represents the post-decision behaviour of undergraduate tobacco consumers, encompassing both the purchase and post-purchase evaluation of tobacco use. This stage reflects how consumers buy and use tobacco products, and how their experiences influence future intentions—whether to continue or quit tobacco consumption.

The mean age of initiation into tobacco use among ATC (Active Tobacco Consumers) is 15.89 years, indicating early exposure and vulnerability during adolescence. Among the various tobacco products, Indian branded cigarettes are the most commonly used (34.49%), followed by Gutkha (31.01%) and Zarda (24.68%). There is also notable consumption of Zial (17.4%), Burmese cigarettes (15.82%), Khaini (11.07%), and Tuibur (10.13%). A significant gender-based difference exists in the choice of tobacco: male respondents tend to prefer smoking forms, whereas female respondents are more inclined toward smokeless tobacco. Most ATC (80.06%) spend ₹30 or less daily on tobacco. The affordability of certain contraband or low-cost alternatives may appeal particularly to heavy users.

Regarding purchase behaviour, 57.28% of ATC prefer to buy single units, while 37.97% purchase full packets. A majority (63.61%) of ATC consume tobacco daily, suggesting high dependency levels. Situational contexts also play a critical role: 65.51% of ATC consume tobacco after meals, 24.68%

during social interactions, and 18.67% in idle moments—highlighting triggers like post-meal cravings, peer influence, and lack of purposeful engagement.

In terms of place of consumption, 48.2% consume tobacco outdoors, 18.35% indoors (home or hostel), and 25.32% anywhere. Despite this, 69.3% avoid consuming tobacco in public places, and 49.37% are concerned about breaking rules when using tobacco in prohibited areas. This indicates a degree of internal conflict or social conformity among users.

Brand loyalty appears weak: 59.5% of ATC either disagree or are unsure about consistently buying the same brand. However, brand loyalty shows a significant association with specific products such as Indian branded cigarettes, Sahda, Gutkha, and Tuibur. The most influential factors in brand choice are ‘easy availability’, ‘flavor and feel’, and ‘low price’.

While only 14.56% of ATC previously stated that tobacco makes them look “cool” or “mature,” a larger proportion (65.51%) do not believe this to be true—suggesting a maturing perspective. Health awareness among users is relatively high: 40.51% of ATC report experiencing health issues due to tobacco, 82.91% acknowledge the risk of cancer, and 87.66% believe it can lead to death.

Despite their consumption, many ATC recognize tobacco’s negative health effects. Around 40% reported using tobacco as a stress reliever. Regarding influence on others, 14.24% have actively encouraged others to consume tobacco, while 39.56% are uncertain but may have indirectly influenced peers. On a positive note, 60.76% have encouraged others to quit. When it comes to quitting intentions:

- 45.57% expressed a willingness to quit in the future.
- 32.28% are currently trying to quit.
- 17.09% have tried and failed in the past.
- Only 5.06% do not intend to quit.

Importantly, 69.3% of ATC believe they can successfully quit tobacco. The most common motivations to quit include the fear of death, and a desire to set a good example for family and future generations. Additionally, graphic health warnings on tobacco packaging were reported to reduce the desire to consume tobacco in 38.61% of ATC.

Exhibit 3.5: Theory of Reasoned Action

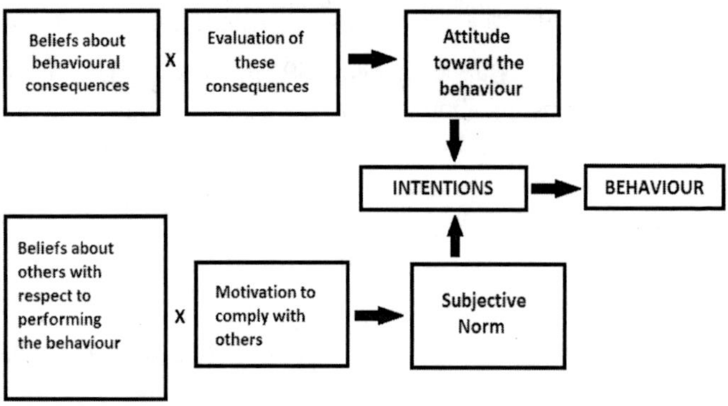

Source: Donovan and Henley (2010), p. 131.

The Theory of Reasoned Action (Fishbein & Ajzen, 1975) (see *Exhibit 3.5*) offers a compelling framework for understanding tobacco consumption behaviour among undergraduate students. According to this theory, behaviour is guided by behavioural intentions, which are influenced by an individual's attitude toward the behaviour and the subjective norms they perceive.

At the age of initiation (15.89 years), students may lack the maturity to fully comprehend the adverse consequences of tobacco use. Their attitudes are shaped by perceived short-term benefits and social approval rather than long-term risks. Simultaneously, peer pressure and societal acceptance create a subjective norm that supports tobacco use. These two factors—positive attitudes and favourable subjective norms—lead to the formation of positive behavioural intentions, which often materialise as actual tobacco consumption. Over time, with the addictive nature of tobacco and consistent environmental reinforcement, this behaviour becomes habitual.

The consumer decision-making process of undergraduate tobacco users in Mizoram, as explained through Schiffman and Kanuk's model and the Theory of Reasoned Action, highlights the interplay between internal psychological factors and external socio-cultural influences. Key take aways include:

- Tobacco marketing, such as point-of-sale displays, attractive packaging, and wide distribution, plays a strong role.
- Social influences, including peer pressure and family use, outweigh general awareness of health risks.
- Motivating factors include personal possession, visual cues, and the appeal of packaging.
- Gender differences exist in the form of tobacco used.
- Many users purchase tobacco in small units and spend modestly.
- Situational triggers include post-meals, socialisation, and boredom.
- Brand loyalty is weak, but factors like availability, flavour, and cost influence choice.
- Despite high consumption, awareness of health risks is high, and many users have intentions or efforts to quit.
- Graphic health warnings have a deterrent effect for some users.

In conclusion, while there is a strong initial inclination toward tobacco consumption among undergraduates, driven by social and psychological factors, there also exists a notable level of awareness and intent to quit, offering scope for effective intervention and policy implementation.

* * * *

To enhance the effectiveness of tobacco control programmes in Mizoram, it is imperative to examine the underlying causes and motivations that sustain tobacco use, particularly among young consumers. The findings of this chapter suggest that tobacco consumption among undergraduate students is influenced by a complex interplay of psychological factors, socio-cultural norms, marketing strategies, and situational triggers. These elements are deeply rooted in the unique lifestyle, socio-economic background, and cultural identity of the people of Mizoram.

Existing research (Mohan et al., 2018) supports the use of culture-based strategies to improve the reach and resonance of tobacco control efforts. Therefore, generic interventions that work in other parts of India may not be equally effective in Mizoram. Instead, a contextual understanding of the consumer decision-making process—from need recognition to post-consumption evaluation—can help design targeted interventions that address the specific factors influencing tobacco behaviour in the region.

A social marketing approach that aligns with the Schiffman and Kanuk (2007) consumer decision-making model can guide this process. For instance:

- External influences such as point-of-sale displays, attractive packaging, and indirect promotions can be curtailed through stricter enforcement of COTPA, 2003.
- Socio-cultural factors, including peer pressure, familial consumption, and social acceptance, can be addressed through locally tailored awareness and de-normalisation campaigns.
- Easy accessibility, especially of low-cost contraband tobacco products, must be regulated through improved supply chain monitoring and legal enforcement.
- Situational triggers—like post-meal cravings, social gatherings, and boredom—should be managed by fostering alternative healthy habits and creating supportive cessation

environments in public spaces, campuses, hostels, and homes.

Such a comprehensive and localised strategy holds greater potential to disrupt the cycle of tobacco addiction and reduce consumption across the population.

Finally, future research and policy should explore comparative analyses based on gender, age, and regional differences to uncover further nuances in tobacco consumption patterns. These insights will be critical for formulating target-specific, evidence-based tobacco control measures that not only reduce prevalence but also shift societal norms in favour of a tobacco-free future.

* * * *

Chapter - 4

Partners in Prevention: State and Civil Society Responses to Tobacco in Mizoram

Tobacco consumption is a complex problem that requires comprehensive long-term strategies with an adequate support system to control its prevalence in society. To build a comprehensive system under which macro- and grassroots-level tobacco control initiatives and programmes can be effectively implemented, the roles played by various government agencies, civil society, NGOs, and social workers are highly important. Civil society, along with other non-governmental organisations and opinion leaders, can act as catalysts for change (Hu et al., 2013). According to Article 4, Guiding Principle No. 7 of the WHO Framework Convention on Tobacco Control (WHO FCTC), "the participation of civil society is essential in achieving the objective of the Convention and its protocols" (WHO, 2003). In Canada, NGOs have played a critical role in advancing tobacco control programmes and policies (Robbins, 2010). Novotny and Mamudu (2008), after examining tobacco control experiences in the United States, concluded that tobacco control activities funded and implemented by government can be most effective when supported by civil society. Reddy and Gupta (2004) highlighted the role of civil society in advancing the agenda of tobacco control in India and made specific recommendations regarding tobacco control initiatives.

NGOs such as Action Against Tobacco (ACT)-India, Green Motherland, Health Related Information Dissemination Amongst Youth-Students Health Action Network (HRIDAY-SHAN), and Voluntary Health Association of India (VHAI) have made valuable efforts including health education, advocacy, litigation, research, focused campaigns, and countering the tobacco industry for tobacco control in India (Reddy & Gupta, 2004). Reddy et al. (2012) also suggested integrating tobacco control into health and development agendas by engaging and creating partnerships across civil society groups from diverse fields such as tobacco control, development, environment, food security, and human rights. Ladusingh et al. (2017) emphasized the urgent need to extend the National Tobacco Control Programme (NTCP) to the community level with involvement of civil societies in Northeast India. In the context of Mizoram, public participation and civil society efforts to reduce tobacco consumption are particularly important, especially because the state is blessed with very active, prominent, and influential civil society organisations such as the Young Mizo Association (YMA), Mizo Hmeichhe Insuihkhawm Pawl (MHIP), Mizo Union Pachhunga (MUP), and the Church, which serve as ideal platforms for tobacco control initiatives (Hatzaw, 2014). Significant opportunities exist for social marketers and policymakers in Mizoram to partner with NGOs such as YMA, MHIP, and MUP on public health matters, given that these organisations hold a central influence in the socio-cultural, economic, and political spheres of Mizoram's population (Laldinliana, 2010).

4.1 Role of Organisations in Tobacco Control in Mizoram

According to the Global Adult Tobacco Survey (GATS) India Report 2016–2017, Mizoram has the second-highest prevalence of tobacco users in the country at 58.7%, more than double the national average of 28.6% (Ministry of Health and Family Welfare [MHFW], 2018). This statistic highlights the ongoing challenges Mizoram faces in its efforts to reduce tobacco use. However, it is encouraging to note that the prevalence of adult tobacco consumption in the state has decreased from 67.2% in GATS 2009–2010. This positive trend can largely be attributed to the dedicated and collaborative efforts of various organisations, government agencies, and social workers committed to making Mizoram tobacco-free.

In light of this development, it is both relevant and necessary to document, examine, and assess the contributions of key stakeholders in tobacco control. Organisations such as the Mizoram State Tobacco Control Cell (MSTC), the Indian Society for Tobacco Control and Health Management Centre (ISTCHMC), as well as influential civil society groups including the Young Mizo Association (YMA), Mizo Hmeichhe Insuihkhawm Pawl (MHIP), Mizo Zirlai Pawl (MZP), and various religious institutions, have all played vital roles in advancing the tobacco control agenda. This chapter draws on an extensive review of existing literature to present qualitative evaluations of these organisations' contributions, suggesting that their efforts have significantly influenced the decline in tobacco use. Nevertheless, there remains a pressing need for broader engagement, deeper collaboration, and improved coordination among these actors to further enhance the effectiveness of tobacco control initiatives in Mizoram.

4.2 The Mizoram State Tobacco Control Society (MSTCS)

The Mizoram State Tobacco Control Society (MSTCS) is the foremost organisation in Mizoram responsible for implementing the *Mizoram State Tobacco Control Programme (MSTCP)* under the *National Tobacco Control Programme (NTCP)*. Established on 30th May 2009, MSTCS operates with a set of objectives aimed at curbing tobacco use in the state (MSTCS, 2018):

1. To undertake all necessary activities toward effective tobacco control in Mizoram.
2. To initiate or collaborate on state, national, or global efforts to strengthen tobacco control.
3. To implement the NTCP at the state level as per central guidelines.
4. To execute the project titled *"Advocacy and Mobilisation for Smoke-Free Mizoram and Effective Tobacco Control*

Implementation in the State", funded by the *Bloomberg Global Initiative to Reduce Tobacco Use*, in collaboration with the *World Lung Foundation* and managed by the *International Union against Tuberculosis and Lung Diseases*.

5. To collaborate with various governmental and non-governmental organisations to combat tobacco use.
6. To undertake any additional responsibilities assigned by the Government of Mizoram from time to time.

MSTCS is registered under the Mizoram Societies Registration Act, 2005 and receives funding from the Bloomberg Initiative to Reduce Tobacco Use, monitored by *The Union South East Asia*, New Delhi. The society is currently chaired by Mr. Lalrinliana Fanai, Principal Secretary (Health and Family Welfare Department), and Ms. Thanhliri Pachuau, Joint Secretary (Health), serves as Vice-Chairperson. Dr. Jane R. Ralte, the State Nodal Officer/Project Officer for 'Smoke-Free Mizoram', also serves as the Member Secretary.

Since April 2009, MSTCS has successfully implemented multiple projects including:

- A two-year initiative on *"Advocacy and Mobilisation for Smoke-Free Mizoram and Effective Tobacco Control"* across all eight districts of Mizoram.
- From July 1, 2011, another two-year project titled *"Advancing Tobacco Control in Mizoram through Capacity Building, Strengthening NTCP, and Effective Enforcement of Tobacco Control Laws"* funded by the Bloomberg Initiative.

To address tobacco-related health issues and support cessation efforts, MSTCS operates several Tobacco Control Cells (TCCs). These are staffed with trained doctors and psychologists who provide Nicotine Replacement Therapy (NRT), counseling, and behavioural interventions. There are 10 functioning TCCs—nine located in district hospitals and one at the Mizoram Cancer Hospital.

The State Tobacco Control Cell (STCC) is based at the State Referral Hospital, Falkawn, and District Tobacco Control Cells

(DTCCs) are located in Aizawl West, Aizawl East, Lunglei, Champhai, Siaha, Serchhip, Kolasib, Mamit, and Lawngtlai. Each DTCC is staffed with a District Consultant, Psychologist/Counselor, Social Worker, and Data Entry Operator. The STCC has a State Consultant, Legal Consultant, Programme Assistant, and a Data Entry Operator (STCC, 2016). Between April 2017 and March 2018, a total of 2,771 clients visited these TCCs, with a quit rate of 24.82%.

MSTCS also partners with several key organisations in Mizoram for joint tobacco control efforts:

- Indian Society on Tobacco and Health (Mizoram Chapter)
- Mizo Zirlai Pawl (Mizo Students' Union)
- Mizo Hmeichhe Insuihkhawm Pawl (Women's Federation of Mizoram)
- Mizoram Journalist Association

Between April 2014 and June 2016, MSTCS conducted 485 anti-tobacco awareness programmes at educational institutions, 137 programmes at churches and community platforms, 151 workshops and trainings, and 75 meetings, talk shows, and other outreach events (MPCC, 2016). The following table summarizes MSTCS's major activities from April 2017 to March 2018 (HFWD, 2018):

Table 4.1: Activities by MSTCS (April 2017 – March 2018)

SN	Activity	No. of Activities	No. of Participants
1.	Training and Sensitisation Workshops	56	3,296
2.	Anti-Tobacco Awareness Campaigns and Programmes	128	11,619
3.	Anti-Tobacco Programmes at Educational Institutions	153	12,227
4.	Others (Meetings, Talk Shows, etc.)	128	673
	Total	**465**	**27,815**

MSTCS actively observes World No Tobacco Day annually with theme-based activities. In 2012, it launched the *Blue Ribbon Campaign* to increase public awareness about the harms of tobacco use (Vanglaini, September 12, 2018). On 30th May 2014, it organised a *Training Programme on Tobacco Control* for legislators, secretaries, and department heads at the Assembly Secretariat Annexe. Similar initiatives were held in 2016 and 2017, including seminars, rallies, and award ceremonies to promote compliance with the *Cigarettes and Other Tobacco Products Act (COTPA), 2003*. The 2017 Mizoram State Anti-Tobacco Day, themed *"Tobacco-Free Sports"*, was held on 11th September. It was attended by representatives of sports associations, with recognition given to outstanding performers in tobacco law compliance. A *No Tobacco Rally* was also conducted on 19th September 2017, funded through Corporate Social Responsibility (CSR) contributions (HFWD, 2018).

On 21st June 2017, the state government launched the HIMNA-MADAT (Mizoram Against Drugs, Alcohol and Tobacco) pilot project, targeting upper primary schools in Aizawl district. It is monitored by the Deputy Commissioner and involves multiple departments and civil society partners. Notably, Thingsul Tlangnuam became the first *smoke-free village* in 2013, followed by Ruantlang village in Champhai district, declared *tobacco-free* in December 2017. On 1st May 2018, the Chief Minister of Mizoram simultaneously launched the *World No Tobacco Month* and the *Tobacco-Free Sports* campaign, in collaboration with the Mizoram State Olympic Association, Indian Society on Tobacco and Health (Mizoram Chapter), and MSTCS (The Morung Express, May 2, 2018). MSTCS has also implemented school-based campaigns such as the *"Save the Future of Children"* event on Children's Day in 2013 (MSTCS, 2013). The 2018 Mizoram State Anti-Tobacco Day, held on 11th September at Aijal Club, saw the Transport Minister, Pu John Rotluangliana, emphasize the success achieved through collaboration between the government and NGOs. Pi Lal Riliani, President of the Indian Society on Tobacco & Health (Mizoram Chapter), also highlighted the environmental impacts of tobacco use (Zonet Chanchin Thar, September 11, 2018).

One of the landmark achievements of sustained advocacy by MSTCS and its partners was the incremental increase in tobacco taxes, initially raised to 20% on 31st May 2014, and subsequently to 30%

by a Cabinet resolution passed on 19th August 2015 (MPCC, 2016). Elizabeth Hatzaw (2014) recognised several notable achievements of MSTCS such as integration of tobacco education into school curricula, inclusion of tobacco-related themes in church services, establishment of tobacco-free communities, capacity building among stakeholders, engagement with civil society organisations (CSOs) and effective interdepartmental networking and resource mobilisation. These multi-pronged efforts have made MSTCS a central figure in Mizoram's tobacco control journey, offering a model of coordinated state and civil society action in public health.

4.3 The Indian Society on Tobacco and Health, Mizoram Chapter (ISTHMC)

The Indian Society on Tobacco and Health, Mizoram Chapter (ISTHMC) is the oldest organisation in Mizoram dedicated to the cause of reducing tobacco consumption and striving toward a tobacco-free state. The society is led by Ms. Lal Riliani, its founding President, who has been a tireless advocate for tobacco control in Mizoram since 1989 (Hmar, 2018). Both Ms. Lal Riliani and Mr. K. Thanseia, the Secretary of ISTHMC, are members of the governing body of the Mizoram State Tobacco Control Society (MSTCS), indicating close collaboration between the two entities.

ISTHMC has played a pioneering role in tobacco control efforts in the state and has consistently coordinated with organisations such as MSTCS to implement various initiatives. Notably, on 31st May 2002, ISTHMC organised Mizoram's first-ever World No Tobacco Day in collaboration with the Tobacco Society of Mizoram and the Department of Health, Government of Mizoram (Hatzaw, 2014). At a time when the state lacked a dedicated tobacco control programme and such initiatives were subsumed under the National Cancer Control Programme (NCCP), ISTHMC partnered with the government to raise awareness among school children and collaborated with churches to deliver anti-tobacco messages (Hatzaw, 2014).

Each year, ISTHMC actively participates in the observance of Mizoram State Anti-Tobacco Day, often in partnership with MSTCS.

On 1st May 2018, the organisation jointly organised an event with the Mizoram State Olympic Association (MSOA) and MSTCS, marking the launch of World No Tobacco Month and the Tobacco Free Sports campaign across the state (The Morung Express, May 2, 2018).

According to Dr. Jane Ralte, the current primary objective of ISTHMC is to "create awareness and achieve smoke-free homes and smoke-free vehicles" (Hmar, 2018). In recognition of their impactful advocacy and public-private collaboration in tobacco control, ISTHMC, along with MSTCS, was honoured with the Regional Director's Appreciation Award as part of the World No Tobacco Day Awards 2015 for the WHO South-East Asia Region (The Economic Times, May 29, 2015).

Despite notable successes in awareness generation, Ms. Lal Riliani has acknowledged that tobacco control efforts have had limited influence on Mizoram's teenagers and youth. She observed that while the campaigns have led to increased public understanding, the addictive nature of tobacco and peer influences make it particularly difficult to reach younger demographics (Kangla Online, November 24, 2016).

4.4 Religious Organisations

Religious organisations can play a significant role in controlling tobacco consumption. On 3rd May 1999, a meeting on *Tobacco and Religion* was held at the WHO headquarters in Geneva, where it was affirmed that "Orthodox Christianity welcomes the Tobacco Free Initiative in the hope that its efforts against tobacco will engage the holistic problem of the need to cure the human person" (WHO, 1999). In the United States, a church-based smoking cessation programme conducted among African-American adults in rural Virginia showed promising results, with a trend towards higher effectiveness among churchgoers and communities with strong religious engagement (Schorling et al., 1997). A later study confirmed that church attendance is associated with lower smoking prevalence, increased cessation, and reduced exposure to environmental tobacco smoke (ETS). The researchers concluded that public health efforts could benefit by collaborating more closely with religious congregations (Hofstetter et al., 2010).

In Mizoram, religious organisations—especially Christian churches—hold significant influence over the socio-cultural behaviour of the Mizo people (Zomuanthanga, 2008). According to Census 2011, 87.1% of Mizoram's population is Christian, with the Presbyterian Church as the largest denomination. Other key Christian denominations in Mizoram include:

- Baptist Church of Mizoram
- United Pentecostal Church
- The Salvation Army
- The Seventh-day Adventist Church
- Kohhran Thianghlim
- Roman Catholic Church
- Lairam Jesus Christ Baptist Church (LIKBK)
- Evangelical Church of Maraland
- Independent Church of India (ICI)
- Evangelical Free Church of India (EFCI)

Churches in Mizoram have traditionally been vocal opponents of alcohol, often playing an active role in influencing public policy. The Mizoram Presbyterian Church Synod, the governing body of the state's largest denomination, strongly opposed the lifting of the Mizoram Liquor Total Prohibition (MLTP) Act, 1995 by the previous Congress government (Zotinkhuma, 2018). The Synod decided that individuals involved in selling liquor or holding permits for consumption would not be allowed to take part in church activities (The Northeast Today, 2015). Churches also organize gospel camps with rehabilitation elements that encourage members to abstain from alcohol, and it is generally believed that church pressure significantly influenced the enactment of the MLTP Act (Zorammuana, 2010).

Despite this, most churches in Mizoram have not demonstrated the same level of activism against tobacco use. Although tobacco consumption remains a significant issue in the region, many churches remained silent on this for a long time (PahrüPou, 2017). While smoking is prohibited within church premises, it is still common to see people smoking just outside church buildings. Some denominations, however, have taken proactive steps. The Presbyterian Church, for example, does not recruit probationary officers who use tobacco, and expects its staff to remain tobacco-free (Zorammuana, 2010). The Seventh-day Adventist Church adopts a broader doctrinal stance, prohibiting the use of substances deemed "unclean," which includes alcohol, tobacco, drugs, and certain meats. Moreover, the Presbyterian Church has introduced tobacco-related themes in its Wednesday Night services, as well as in annual observances like Health Sunday, Leprosy Sunday, and Cancer Sunday (Hatzaw, 2014).

Given that church services in Mizoram cater to distinct groups such as children, youth, and women, they offer a strategic platform for targeted tobacco control interventions (Hatzaw, 2014). The significance of this role is highlighted by the involvement of Rev. Lalhmuchhuaka, Chairman of the Mizoram Kohhran Hruaitute Committee (MKHC)—a coalition of 16 major churches in the state—who also serves on the governing board of the Mizoram State Tobacco Control Society (MSTCS).

In May 2018, a Training of Trainers (ToT) programme for church leaders on substance abuse prevention was conducted under Project Himna-MADAT (Mizoram Against Drugs, Alcohol & Tobacco) at the Administrative Training Institute, showcasing the potential of religious collaboration in health promotion (Vanglaini, May 29, 2018).

4.5 Other Prominent Non-Government Organisations in Mizoram

Mizoram has several influential NGOs like the Young Mizo Association (YMA), Mizo Hmeichhe Insuihkhawm Pawl (MHIP), and Mizo Zirlai Pawl (MZP), known for their strong community presence. While they do not primarily focus on tobacco control, these organisations have contributed significantly to related public health, education, and social awareness efforts. They have also collaborated with the Government, MSTCS, and ISTHMC in various tobacco control initiatives, supporting awareness and advocacy at the grassroots level. The following section highlights some of their key roles in tobacco control in Mizoram.

4.5.1 Young Mizo Association (YMA)

The Young Mizo Association, popularly known as YMA, is the largest voluntary civil organisation in Mizoram. Among all NGOs in the state, YMA is recognised as the oldest, largest, and most influential social organisation (Chawngthanmawii, 2014). It is registered under the Societies Registration Act (Act XXI of 1860) with Registration No. SR4 of 1977 (Mizoram State National Informatics Centre, n.d.). Established on 15th June 1935 in Aizawl, it was originally named the Young Lushai Association. The organisation was renamed the Young Mizo Association on 7th October 1947 (YMA, 2012). Today, YMA comprises 5 sub-headquarters, 47 group YMAs, 772 branches, and over 400,000 members spread across Mizoram and neighbouring states such as Assam, Manipur, Meghalaya, Nagaland, and Tripura (YMA, 2012).

The YMA is widely acknowledged for successfully replacing the traditional bachelor's dormitory system called the *Zawlbuk*[1], which was an integral part of Mizo society and culture, renowned for its strict civic values and dedicated community service. In many ways, the modern YMA continues to uphold these core values. The organisation operates under three main mottos (YMA, 2012):

1. Good use/ Proper utilisation of leisure time.
2. Reverence for a good Christian life.
3. Striving towards a holistic development of the Mizo society.

Since its inception, one of YMA's primary roles has been assisting the poor and needy. Their most common and dedicated service is

1. The traditional system of Mizo bachelor's dormitory, *Zawlbuk*, served as a vital institution for education, socialisation, security, and community service, shaping young men into responsible, skilled, and community-oriented individuals.

providing support during deaths in the community (Mizoram State National Informatics Centre, n.d.). YMA is also known for its prompt rescue and relief efforts during natural calamities such as landslides. The organisation runs Adult Education Centres across Mizoram, contributing significantly to the state's high literacy rate. It has established the Youth Development and Training Centre (*Zawlbuk Ram*) at Thingsulthliah and manages over 250 public libraries throughout Mizoram.

Since 1974, YMA has spearheaded the 'Green Mizoram' project, organizing statewide tree plantation drives. The organisation also regularly conducts cleanliness campaigns, health and sanitation awareness programmes, and has constructed numerous public toilets in towns and villages. For its exceptional contributions to environmental conservation, YMA received the 'Indira Gandhi Paryavaran Puruskar' in 1993 from the Government of India (Mizoram State National Informatics Centre, n.d.).

YMA also actively preserves Mizo culture and heritage by organizing mass participation events in sports, social, and cultural activities. A notable achievement of YMA is its role as a voluntary organisation ensuring free and fair elections during State Assembly and Parliamentary elections. The Government of Mizoram awarded YMA the 'Excellence Service Award' for three consecutive years from 1988 to 1990 (Mizoram State National Informatics Centre, n.d.).

The organisation strongly campaigns against drug and alcohol abuse, opposing the use and sale of alcohol in Mizoram. From 2004 to 2008, "Fight against Intoxicants" was YMA's annual theme. Under this initiative, the Supply Reduction Service (SRS) and Demand Reduction Service (DRS) squads were established. In May 2010, the Central YMA formed the Central Anti-Drugs Squad to combat drugs and drug trafficking (Zorammuana, 2010). Currently, YMA runs special programmes on HIV/AIDS awareness, conducting seminars, campaigns, and distributing educational materials to inform the public about the disease (Mizoram State National Informatics Centre, n.d.).

Laldinliana (2010) observed that while YMA's proactive efforts have led to a reduction in drug abuse in recent years, the state continues to struggle with the issue of tobacco consumption. Interestingly, in the late 1930s, YMA initially promoted the use of Mizo tobacco with the slogan that it was a cheaper alternative to cigarettes, aiming to preserve Mizo tradition (Chawngthanmawii, 2014). However, YMA has since become increasingly aware of the harmful effects of tobacco and now supports government initiatives against tobacco use. Mr. Vanlalruata, the General Secretary of Central YMA, is a member of the governing body of the Mizoram State Tobacco Control Society (MSTCS). In partnership with MSTCS, YMA organised tobacco awareness programmes in five schools on 5th June 2009 (Zorammuana, 2010). Additionally, several YMA branches and village councils have imposed bans on the sale of gutkha in their areas (WebIndia123, Jun 20, 2010).

4.5.2 Mizo Hmeichhe Insuihkhawm Pawl (MHIP)

Mizo Hmeichhe Insuihkhawm Pawl (MHIP), which literally means *"binding the women together"*, is the largest women's organisation in Mizoram. Its headquarters is located in Aizawl. Established on 6th July 1974, MHIP is registered under Registration No. 5 of 1977, Society Act 1860 (Act XXI of 1960). The organisation has branches (sub-headquarters) in all districts of Mizoram and is active in 16 blocks, with 12 joint headquarters and 740 local branches across the state (Hanghal, 2014).

MHIP is founded on the Mizo cultural ethos of *Tlawmngaihna*—a spirit of selfless service and community welfare without the expectation of personal gain. Its core objective is to build a society where every individual is cared for, regardless of caste or creed (NIC, n.d.). The key activities of MHIP include the followings:

1. Advocating for women's rights and development in Mizoram, including the review of Mizo Customary Laws to protect women's legal and social rights.
2. Combating violence and atrocities against women, including rape, murder, gender-based violence, and domestic abuse.

3. Offering family counseling, support, and guidance to single mothers, divorcees, and women in distress.
4. Providing financial or material aid to destitute women and children from economically weaker sections of society.
5. Conducting leadership, vocational, and entrepreneurship training to empower women.
6. Organizing awareness campaigns and social events focusing on education, health, hygiene, and overall well-being.

Beyond its role in women's rights and empowerment, MHIP has made noteworthy contributions to health awareness in Mizoram. It has worked among vulnerable groups such as injecting drug users, female sex workers, and migrant labourers to prevent the spread of HIV/AIDS. MHIP also facilitated advocacy meetings on HIV/AIDS involving NGOs, community-based organisations (CBOs), and church leaders in Lawngtlai (Indian NGOs, n.d.).

Under the sponsorship of the Department of Health, MHIP implemented family planning programmes and medicine distribution in rural areas, covering over 400 villages. In March 2015, its Falkawn Branch, in collaboration with the State Referral Hospital, organised a sensitisation programme on non-communicable diseases and hosted a free medical clinic at the hospital (Northeast Today, March 16, 2015).

Ms. Lalthlamuani, President of MHIP, is also a member of the governing body of the Mizoram State Tobacco Control Society (MSTCS). MHIP has actively participated in anti-tobacco initiatives, including squad drives and joint enforcement efforts with departments such as Legal Metrology, Food and Drug Administration, Traffic Police, and CID (Crime) (HFWD, 2018).

MHIP also led a state-wide campaign against gutkha, during which leaders of various MHIP branches in Aizawl pledged to combat the issue and ban its sale in their respective areas. On MHIP Day, observed on 6th July 2014, the then Health Minister of Mizoram, Mr. Lal Thanzara, commended MHIP for its strong campaign against tobacco products like gutkha. He highlighted the harmful impact of products like *Tiranga*—a commonly used brand of gutkha in Mizoram—on the health of the youth (Hueiyen News Service, July 6, 2014). In 2015, MHIP, in collaboration with MSTCS, also organised a seminar on tobacco control and gutkha products (Vanglaini, July 24, 2015).

4.5.3 Mizoram Journalists Association (MJA)

Mizoram Journalists Association (MJA) is a welfare organisation representing working journalists in Mizoram. Headquartered in Aizawl, the association was founded in 1972, with former Chief Minister of Mizoram, Mr. Lalthanhawla, serving as its founding president (The Telegraph, November 15, 2012). The current president of MJA is Mr. C. Lalrambuatsaiha. The MJA is widely acknowledged for its significant contributions to the growth and development of journalism in Mizoram. As Dr. C. Lalmuansangkimi (2015) observed, "The presence and well-organised functioning of the Mizoram Journalists Association (MJA) may be attributed with the booming of Print Journalism in Mizoram."

Over the years, MJA has collaborated with the Department of Health and the Mizoram State Tobacco Control Society (MSTCS) on several health-related awareness campaigns, including tobacco control initiatives. Mr. Vanlalrema Vantawl, a former president of MJA, also serves as a member of the governing body of MSTCS. In December 2015, MJA, in association with MSTCS and with support from *The Union*—an international voluntary scientific organization—organised a one-day Media Workshop on Tobacco Control at the Aizawl Press Club (Northeast Today, December 14, 2015). The workshop aimed to sensitize media professionals on the rising public health challenges posed by increasing tobacco consumption in the state. Further, on 27th March 2019, the Lunglei District Tobacco Control Cell (DTCC) conducted a Training on Tobacco Control for members of MJA and the Department of Information and Public Relations (I&PR) at the I&PR Conference Hall in Lunglei. The programme was chaired by Dr. S. R. Ngurchamliana, Medical Superintendent and District Nodal Officer of the National Tobacco Control Programme (NTCP) (Lalremruati, 2019).

4.5.4 Mizo Zirlai Pawl (MZP)

The Mizo Zirlai Pawl (MZP) is the largest and apex student organisation in Mizoram. Its origins can be traced back to 27th October 1935, with the establishment of the Lushai Students Association (LSA) in Shillong. On 1st September 1946, the LSA was reconstituted as the Mizo Zirlai Pawl (MZP), as it is known today (Zate, 2017). The organisation is registered under the Indian Societies Registration Act with SR No. 35 of 1969–70. Since 2008, MZP has observed October 27th as "*Zirlaite Ni*" (Students' Day) in Mizoram, commemorating its founding.

The MZP currently maintains 12 headquarters, including one each in Tripura and Manipur, 50 sub-headquarters, and several branches both within and outside Mizoram. It also has eight affiliated tribe-based student organisations under its umbrella. The motto of MZP is *'Ṭanrual hi Chakna'* ("Union is Strength") and its guiding theme is *'Mizo zirlaite kan ram leh hnam tan'* ("Serve for the Mizo Nation").

According to Zate (2017), the main aims and objectives of MZP are as follows:

- To safeguard the rights and unity of all Mizo students;
- To prepare Mizo youth to become responsible and contributing citizens of Zoram;
- To promote unity among all Mizo communities and advocate for the formation of an independent Mizo state encompassing all historically Mizo-inhabited territories;
- To combat and prevent corruption in Mizoram;
- To preserve and uphold traditional Mizo values.

The MZP has actively participated in various socio-political and developmental issues in the state. Notably, MZP representatives, along with members of other NGOs, attended the first meeting of the State Level Coordination Committee on Tobacco Control held on 29th July 2014. The objective of this committee is to enhance the enforcement of various provisions under the Cigarettes and

Other Tobacco Products Act (COTPA) and to strengthen the fight against tobacco use in the state. During the meeting, the Committee Chairperson, L. Tochhong, appealed for coordinated efforts from all stakeholders—including government departments and NGOs—to intensify actions to curb tobacco consumption (Sinlung, July 29, 2014).

Subsequently, on 29th August 2014, the MZP, in collaboration with the Mizoram State Tobacco Control Society (MSTCS), organised the Youth MPOWER Summit at the Tourist Lodge in Chaltlang. At the summit, Dr. Jane R. Ralte, State Nodal Officer of MSTCS, presented the different components of the WHO-recommended MPOWER strategies for tobacco control. Participants engaged in discussions on practical approaches and innovative ideas for implementing these strategies effectively across Mizoram (MPCC, 2016).

4.6 Implementation of NTCP & COTPA in Mizoram

While national tobacco control efforts in India are anchored in frameworks like COTPA, 2003 and the National Tobacco Control Programme (NTCP), their effectiveness ultimately relies on state-level execution. In Mizoram—where tobacco consumption rates are among the highest in the country—focused implementation of these legal and policy measures has been especially crucial. This section explores India's regulatory framework for tobacco control and how NTCP and COTPA have been implemented in the state, with particular attention to institutional arrangements, enforcement mechanisms, awareness initiatives, and cessation services.

4.6.1 Legal Foundations of Tobacco Control in India

India's regulatory framework for tobacco control has evolved significantly over the decades. The initial legislative step was taken in 1975 through the Cigarettes (Regulation of Production, Supply and Distribution) Act, which mandated statutory health warnings on all cigarette packages and advertisements (Shimkhada & Peabody, 2003; Reddy & Gupta, 2004; Mishra et al., 2012). However, as tobacco-related health concerns escalated, the need for a more robust and comprehensive legal framework became apparent.

This led to the introduction of the Cigarettes and Other Tobacco Products (Prohibition of Advertisement and Regulation of Trade and Commerce, Production, Supply and Distribution) Act (COTPA), 2003, which came into force on 18th May 2003 (Mishra et al., 2012). COTPA is applicable to all tobacco products as listed in its Schedule and extends across India, including the state of Jammu and Kashmir. Key provisions of COTPA, as summarised by Mishra et al. (2012), include:

- Prohibition of smoking in public places, including indoor workplaces (effective from 2nd October 2008).
- Ban on tobacco advertisements, both direct and indirect (with limited exception for point-of-sale displays).
- Prohibition of sale to and by minors, and restrictions on sales within 100 yards of educational institutions.
- Mandatory health warnings in English and one Indian language, with pictorial depictions.
- Regulation of tar and nicotine content, including mandatory disclosure on packaging.

In addition, Section 4 of COTPA and the accompanying Prohibition of Smoking in Public Places Rules, 2008, seek to protect the public from Second-Hand Smoke (SHS) exposure through comprehensive bans on smoking in public areas.

While COTPA does not ban the use or production of tobacco products outright, the Food Safety and Standards (Prohibition and Restrictions on Sales) Regulations, 2011, notified under the Food Safety and Standards Act, 2006, prohibit the production, sale, storage, and distribution of food products containing tobacco or nicotine, such as gutkha, with effect from 1st August 2011.

4.6.2 Objectives and Structure of National Tobacco Control Programme

In response to the growing burden of tobacco-related morbidity and mortality, the Ministry of Health and Family Welfare, Government of India launched the National Tobacco Control Programme (NTCP) in the financial year 2007–08 (Jhanjee, 2011; Kaur & Jain, 2011). The NTCP was developed as a strategic public health intervention to strengthen tobacco control efforts across the country in alignment with the provisions of COTPA, 2003.

The primary objectives of NTCP are as follows:

(a) To create awareness about the harmful effects of tobacco consumption and about existing tobacco control laws.

(b) To reduce the production and supply of tobacco products.

(c) To ensure effective implementation of the provisions laid out in the Cigarettes and Other Tobacco Products Act (COTPA), 2003.

(d) To assist individuals in quitting tobacco use through the establishment and operation of Tobacco Cessation Centers (TCCs).

To achieve these objectives, the programme focuses on several key areas of intervention:

- Training and capacity-building for health workers, social workers, NGOs, school teachers, and enforcement officers.
- Information, Education and Communication (IEC) activities aimed at public awareness.
- School-based programmes to promote tobacco-free lifestyles among children and adolescents.
- Monitoring and enforcement of tobacco control laws, particularly the provisions under COTPA.
- Coordination with Panchayati Raj Institutions (PRIs) to facilitate grassroots-level implementation of tobacco control initiatives.
- Establishment and strengthening of cessation services, including access to pharmacological treatment at the district level.

At the national level, the implementation of NTCP is overseen by the National Tobacco Control Cell (NTCC). The NTCC is responsible for policy formulation, strategic planning, coordination, implementation, monitoring, and evaluation of programme components. It operates under the direct supervision of programme heads from the Ministry of Health and Family Welfare—typically the Joint Secretary or Director. Technical guidance is provided by designated officers from the Directorate General of Health Services, such as the Deputy Director General (DDG) or Chief Medical Officer (CMO). Additionally, the NTCC is supported by a team of specialised consultants working in thematic areas such as Policy, National Coordination, Legal Affairs, and IEC.

4.6.3 Mizoram State Tobacco Control Programme (MSTCP)

The Government of Mizoram has localised the National Tobacco Control Programme (NTCP) through the creation of the Mizoram State Tobacco Control Programme (MSTCP). To facilitate its implementation, the state established the Mizoram State Tobacco Control Society (MSTCS), which oversees the operation of one State Tobacco Control Cell (STCC) and nine District Tobacco Control Cells (DTCCs) across the state.

In recent years, the Government of Mizoram has undertaken several proactive measures to strengthen tobacco control. Notably, since 2014, the state has been observing September 11 each year as 'Mizoram State Anti-Tobacco Day', making it the first state in India to dedicate an official day to tobacco control awareness (MPCC, 2016).

Mizoram has also demonstrated administrative innovation and legal rigor in enforcing COTPA provisions. It remains the only state in India to authorize all ranks of police personnel to enforce Section 4 (prohibition of smoking in public places) and Section 6(a) and 6(b) (prohibition of sale to and by minors, and within 100 yards of educational institutions). Additionally, Mizoram was the first state to establish an Anti-Tobacco Squad (Hmar, 2018).

In furtherance of Section 4 enforcement, the General Administration Department issued a government notification on 21st April 2017, prohibiting smoking in all public and government office spaces. The order directed all departments to strictly fine offenders, display 'No Smoking' signage and complaint boards, and establish a Tobacco Control Team within each office (HFWD, 2018).

To comply with Article 5.3 of the WHO Framework Convention on Tobacco Control (FCTC)—which mandates protection of public health policies from tobacco industry interference—a special committee was constituted on 20th May 2016. This multi-departmental committee comprises representatives from Health and Family Welfare, Taxation, Trade and Commerce, Law and Judicial, CID (Crime), Information and Public Relations (I&PR), and NTCP (MPCC, 2016).

Mizoram's geographical location, sharing international borders with Myanmar and Bangladesh, has made it a vulnerable market for contraband cigarettes. In response, a Joint Task Force was established on 3rd May 2016 to address the influx of illegal tobacco products. This task force has conducted several joint enforcement drives across districts, resulting in the seizure of 2,501 cartons and 722 packets of contraband cigarettes, including brands such as *Valiant*, *Hummer*, *Farstar*, and *Winbody* (MPCC, 2016).

Complementing these efforts, the Joint Controller of Legal Metrology issued an order on 27th July 2017, directing Legal Metrology Inspectors to carry out frequent and intensive inspections targeting illegal cigarettes across all districts. Subsequently, 471 Anti-Tobacco Squad drives were conducted across Mizoram, registering 494 offenders under COTPA, 2003. Joint enforcement operations were also carried out in collaboration with departments and organisations such as Legal Metrology, Food and Drug Administration, Traffic Police, CID (Crime), and MHIP (Mizo Hmeichhe Insuihkhawm Pawl) (HFWD, 2018).

On 11th September, 2015, the Government of Mizoram issued a notification to completely ban the sale of tobacco products in single sticks, loose, or outside their original packaging without the pictorial health warnings as mandated by the *Cigarettes and Other Tobacco Products Act (COTPA), 2003* (MPCC, 2016). Following this, on 7th August, 2017, the Police Headquarters instructed the DIGs of

Northern and Southern Ranges to include COTPA violations as a regular item in monthly crime review meetings at district, range, and state levels (HFWD, 2018).

On 18th July, 2017, the Director General of Police (DGP), Mizoram launched officially approved "No Smoking" stickers, to be displayed in all public transport vehicles as per directions from the State Transport Authority. Subsequently, the Transport Department issued a notification on 18th August, 2017, mandating all public transport vehicles to comply with the *Prohibition of Smoking in Public Places Rules, 2008*. It required the prominent display of "No Smoking" signs, and any violation would attract a fine up to ₹500 under Section 179 (1) of the Motor Vehicle Act, 1988 (HFWD, 2018).

In line with these enforcement efforts, the Mizoram State Tobacco Control Society (MSTCS) in collaboration with the Aizawl City Traffic Police organised the "COTPA Enforcement Week Kick-Off Programme cum Release of Christmas Card for Drivers" on 18th December, 2017. This campaign involved distribution of Christmas-themed educational materials and enforcement drives among public transport operators (HFWD, 2018). Moreover, joint squad drives involving traffic personnel and anti-tobacco squads have been carried out across districts to ensure compliance with tobacco control laws.

Specific actions have also been taken against the use and sale of hookah in public eateries. The Aizawl District Anti-Tobacco Squad, along with the Food Safety Authority, conducted joint enforcement drives against such establishments. Furthermore, the Deputy Commissioner of Aizawl District issued an order prohibiting the manufacture of Tuibur at Lungli River, Salem Veng, a residential area. Though this order was challenged in court by Mr. Dengvunga and five others, the Gauhati High Court, Mizoram Bench, dismissed their PIL, upholding the enforcement action.

Encouragingly, in December 2017, Ruantlang Village in Champhai District was declared a 'Tobacco-Free Village' by the Additional Deputy Commissioner of Champhai, after full compliance with all sections of COTPA was observed (HFWD, 2018). From April 2014 to June 2016, a total of 353 anti-tobacco squad drives were conducted, leading to the identification of 1701 offenders, and the seizure of 3135 cartons and 1366 packets of foreign cigarettes, mainly in violation of Section 7 of *COTPA, 2003*, which prohibits the sale of tobacco products without health warnings (MPCC, 2016).

The implementation of the State Tobacco Control Programme has yielded measurable progress as evident from the comparison of GATS-1 and GATS-2, where overall tobacco use prevalence decreased from 67.2% to 58.7%. Likewise, second-hand smoke exposure at home dropped from 96.5% to 84.1%, and exposure at the workplace fell from 64.6% to 44.4%. This suggests a growing awareness among the public regarding the risks of smoking in shared environments.

However, challenges remain. As Ladusingh et al. (2017) observe, *COTPA* has not been very effective in controlling tobacco use among teens and youth in northeast India. Similarly, Lal et al. (2015) argue that efforts to restrict the sale of tobacco to underage users need significant strengthening. In Mizoram, despite governmental initiatives, implementation gaps persist. For instance, primary data indicates that 89.8% of 500 student respondents reported the availability of tobacco products within 100 meters/yards[1] of college campuses, in direct violation of Section 6 of COTPA, 2003, which prohibits such sales near educational institutions.

One of the major enforcement hurdles is the widespread availability of contraband cigarettes, especially those of Chinese and Myanmar origin, which are easily accessible and often cheaper than Indian brands. While the Legal Metrology Department has conducted inspections to curb this issue, success has been limited and short-lived. Dr. Jane Ralte observed that although the strict enforcement of COTPA has contributed to a reduction in adult tobacco consumption—from 67.2% in 2009–10 to 58.7% in 2016–17—the widespread availability of inexpensive foreign cigarettes, particularly those manufactured in

1. 1 yard is equal to 0.9144 meters. For the ease of better understanding by respondent students, they were asked if tobacco products are available within 100 meter (instead of 100 yard as per COTPA, 2003) radius around their college campuses.

China, continues to impede progress. She noted that due to rising prices of domestically produced tobacco products aimed at curbing usage and preventing cancer, individuals from lower-income groups are increasingly turning to these more affordable foreign alternatives (Karmakar, 2018).

Exhibit 4.1: Public Notification on Tobacco Packaging

ATTENTION!

Tobacco product Manufacturers, Distributors, Retailers and Importers!

The Central Government has notified the new specified health warnings vide G.S.R 331 (E) of Gazette Notification dated 3rd April, 2018 for mandatory display on all tobacco product packages covering at least 85% of the principal display area. These rules shall come into force on 1st September 2018. There shall be one common specified health warning for both smoking and smokeless forms of tobacco products.

Image-1: This shall be valid for a period of twelve months from 1st September, 2018. The word "TOBACCO CAUSES CANCER" shall appear in white font colour on a red background and the words "QUIT TODAY CALL 1800-11-2356" shall appear in white font colour on a black background.

Image-2: This shall come into effect from 1st September, 2019. The word " TOBACCO CAUSES PAINFUL DEATH" shall appear in white font colour on a red background and the words "QUIT TODAY CALL 1800-11-2356" shall appear in white font colour on a black background.

Image-1

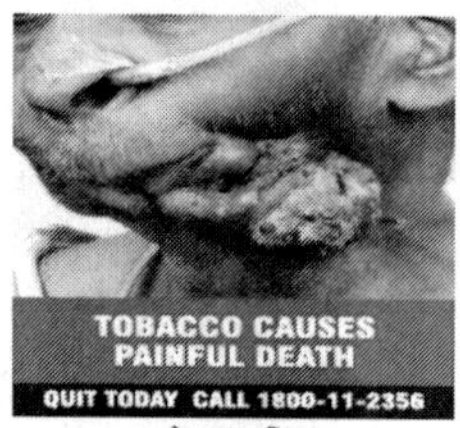

Image-2

The pictorial health warning and textual health warning shall be printed with four colours with printing resolution of minimum 300 DPI (Dots per inch). Their font type and colour shall be exactly as prescribed.

All tobacco products manufactured or imported or packaged on or after 1st September, 2018 shall display Image-1 and those manufactured or imported or packaged on or after 1st September, 2019 shall display Image-2.

Any person engaged directly or indirectly in the production, supply, import or distribution of cigarettes or any tobacco products shall ensure that all tobacco product packages shall have the specified health warnings exactly as prescribed.

Violation of the above mentioned provision is a punishable offence with imprisonment or fine as prescribed in Section 20 of the Cigarettes and Other Tobacco Products (Prohibition of Advertisement and Regulation of Trade and Commerce, Production, Supply and Distribution) Act, 2003.

The images, details of the specified health warnings and the Rules are available at www.mohfw.nic.in . The open files of the images may also be obtained from the Ministry by making a request at **ntcp.mohfw@gmail.com and/or 011-23062868**

Note: The existing specified health warnings on tobacco product packages shall continue till the 31st day of August, 2018.

Ministry of Health & Family Welfare Government of India

All forms of tobacco are addictive and deadly – QUIT TOBACCO USE TODAY

To quit tobacco call 1800 11 2356 or give a missed call on 011-22901701

Source: Ministry of Health and Family Welfare, Government of India (n.d.).

Despite various regulatory efforts, there remains a significant and persistent presence of contraband cigarettes, primarily smuggled from Myanmar, in local markets across Mizoram. These illicit products pose a major challenge to the effective implementation of the Cigarettes and Other Tobacco Products Act (COTPA), not only due to their widespread availability and lower prices, but also because they fail to comply with mandated health communication standards. According to the Cigarettes and Other Tobacco Products (Packaging and Labelling) Second Amendment Rules, 2018, it is mandatory for all tobacco manufacturers, importers, distributors, and retailers to ensure that 85% of the principal display area of tobacco product packaging is covered with pictorial health warnings (PHWs) (Exhibit 4.1). The World Health Organisation (WHO) emphasizes that such graphic warnings play a vital role in discouraging youth and young adults from initiating tobacco use, promoting cessation among current users, and reducing exposure to secondhand smoke (Mansour & Bakhsh, 2017).

Exhibit 4.2: Warning Displayed on Indian and Contraband Cigarette Packaging

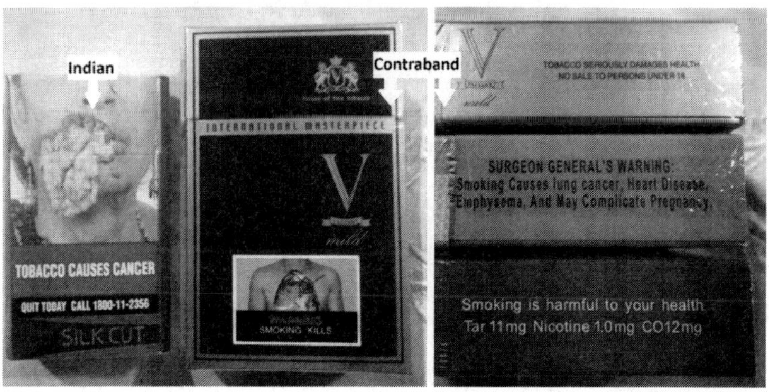

This measure holds particular significance in Mizoram. Primary data from the present study reveals that 38.61% of active tobacco consumers reported a decreased desire to consume tobacco or smoke upon viewing pictorial health warnings on tobacco packaging. A comprehensive study by Raute et al. (2009) also affirmed the effectiveness of pictorial health warnings in the Indian context. International evidence also strongly supports the effectiveness of such warnings. For instance, Thailand, which employs PHWs rated highest by WHO, also recorded the highest proportion of smokers considering quitting due to these warnings (Song et al., 2013). However, the packaging of contraband cigarettes available in Mizoram is largely non-compliant with these requirements. They often lack standardized and explicit pictorial warnings, and the textual warnings—where present—are inconsistently formatted, appears in smaller font size and lack adequate visibility to effectively influence consumer behaviour (Exhibit 4.2).

Dr. Jane Ralte notes that Chinese tobacco producers have adapted their strategies by beginning to include 80% pictorial health warnings on their packaging in response to enforcement measures and product seizures carried out under COTPA regulations. (Karmakar, 2018). However, the challenge persists due to regulatory loopholes. Notably, cigarettes are currently permitted for import under the Indo-Myanmar Trade Agreement of 1995. In response, the Mizoram State Tobacco Control Cell has formally appealed to the central government to remove tobacco products from the list of permissible items under this trade agreement (Karmakar, 2018).

In addition to contraband imports, domestically produced generic tobacco products such as Zial, Sahda, and Tuibur also pose significant challenges to regulatory enforcement. These products typically lack the mandatory graphic health warnings required under COTPA, 2003. The continued circulation of such unregulated and improperly labeled tobacco products undermines the objectives of the Cigarettes and Other Tobacco Products Act and weakens the implementation of the National Tobacco Control Programme in Mizoram. These gaps not only hinder compliance but also dilute public health messaging and reduce the overall effectiveness of tobacco control efforts in the state.

* * * *

Despite being a committed member of the WHO Framework Convention on Tobacco Control (FCTC), India has been slow in ratifying and implementing the FCTC Protocol (Barik et al., 2016). This delay has, to some extent, resulted in fragmented and state-specific approaches rather than a cohesive national strategy. The implications of this sluggish progress are particularly evident in Mizoram, where the persistently high prevalence of tobacco use continues to pose significant socio-economic and public health challenges, thereby hindering the broader developmental goals of the state.

However, based on the recent trends in tobacco consumption prevalence and a qualitative assessment of the interventions by various organisations, it can be concluded that Mizoram has made modest yet noteworthy progress in tobacco control over the past few years. The adult tobacco use rate declined from 67.2% in 2009–2010 to 58.7% in 2016–2017, marking a significant reduction. This positive development can be largely credited to the proactive efforts of key organisations such as the Mizoram State Tobacco Control Society (MSTCS) and the Indian Society for Tobacco and Health in Mizoram Chapter (ISTHMC), whose initiatives have played a central role in advancing the state's tobacco control agenda.

It is also worth acknowledging that Ms. Lal Riliani, President of the Indian Society for Tobacco and Health, Mizoram Chapter (ISTHMC), played a pivotal role in drawing early and much-needed attention to the high prevalence of tobacco use as a pressing public health issue in Mizoram. Similarly, Dr. Jane Ralte, the State Nodal Officer for the National Tobacco Control Programme (NTCP), has provided visionary leadership in steering the state's tobacco control initiatives. The contributions of other influential civil society organisations such as the Young Mizo Association (YMA), Mizo Hmeichhe Insuihkhawm Pawl (MHIP), Mizo Zirlai Pawl (MZP), and the Church have also been significant; however, their engagement has yet to reach its full potential. Greater involvement from the academic community—particularly educators in schools and higher education institutions—is equally essential to strengthen the state's tobacco control framework. Enhanced collaboration, sustained engagement, and coordinated efforts among these various stakeholders are critical for the effective implementation of targeted tobacco control strategies in Mizoram. Nonetheless, the persistent and widespread availability of contraband tobacco products, especially illicit cigarettes, continues to pose a major obstacle to comprehensive tobacco control in the state.

* * * *

Chapter - 5

Towards a Tobacco-Free Mizoram: Challenges, Opportunities, and the Road Ahead

The journey towards a tobacco-free Mizoram is complex, marked by deep-rooted cultural practices, persistent patterns of addiction, and the evolving dynamics of public health governance. While the prevalence of tobacco consumption remains alarmingly high, recent trends offer a glimmer of hope. As pointed earlier, Mizoram witnessed a notable decline in tobacco use, from 67.2% to 58.7%, along with a reduction in exposure to secondhand smoke both at home and in the workplace. These figures, though encouraging, still position Mizoram among the states with the highest rates of tobacco usage in India—a sobering reminder that much work remains to be done.

This final chapter brings together the key insights and arguments explored throughout the book. It offers a synthesized reflection on the factors influencing tobacco-related attitudes and behaviours, the decision-making processes of consumers, and the critical roles played by civil society and state mechanisms. Building on these insights, the chapter outlines the major challenges that hinder progress, identifies emerging opportunities for effective intervention, and proposes a strategic, multi-stakeholder roadmap toward a tobacco-free future. As Mizoram navigates this path, a coordinated, culturally sensitive, and sustained approach will be essential to transform public health outcomes and foster a healthier society.

5.1 Drivers of Tobacco Consumption in Mizoram

The primary data from this study reveals that 63.2% of undergraduate student respondents in Mizoram are currently active tobacco consumers—a figure that is deeply concerning. This high prevalence cannot be attributed to a singular cause; instead, it stems from a complex interplay of socio-economic, cultural, and psychological factors that encourage, reinforce, and sustain tobacco use among the youth.

A distinct pattern emerges when comparing the two colleges studied—Pachhunga University College in Aizawl district and Government Saiha College in Siaha district. These two contrasting districts differ significantly in terms of population density, economic development[1], and levels of urbanization. The data indicates an active tobacco consumption (ATC) rate of 59.75% in Aizawl compared to a much higher 69.49% in Siaha. This regional disparity suggests that local socio-economic conditions, including the relative effectiveness of tobacco control initiatives, may influence consumption patterns.

This local trend reflects a broader global pattern, where tobacco use is declining in more economically developed regions but increasing in less developed areas (Brandt, 2007). Within Mizoram, income levels also appear to affect tobacco behaviour. While affordability can sustain consumption among those with higher disposable income, students with economic constraints are more likely to cite cost as a motivation to quit. Notably, 69.3% of active users reported that the cost of tobacco is high, and those who are financially independent or only partially dependent were more inclined toward tobacco use compared to fully dependent students. These observations align with findings summarised by the World Health Organisation (WHO, n.d.), which highlight that price and consumer disposable income are the two most significant determinants of tobacco demand globally. According to the WHO, an increase in tobacco prices leads to a

1. Both Siaha and Lawngtlai districts have been identified as backward regions by the Ministry of Panchayati Raj, Government of India. As a result, they have been receiving financial assistance under the Backward Regions Grant Fund (BRGF) since 2009 to address regional imbalances in development.

decline in consumption regardless of a country's income level, while a rise in income tends to increase tobacco use, particularly in low-income settings. Moreover, as income grows, consumers often shift their preference toward higher-priced tobacco products.

From a cultural and psychological standpoint, the Social Learning Theory (Bandura, 1977) provides an important lens for analysis. Behavior is often learned through observation and social reinforcement, and in Mizoram, family and peer influences play a significant role in shaping tobacco use among young people. The data shows that 83.54% of active users and 80.49% of past users had family members who also consumed tobacco, indicating that exposure to tobacco use within the household may normalise and encourage similar behaviours. Chapter 3 also established a statistically significant association between family tobacco use and user category, further emphasizing this intergenerational influence.

Beyond family, peer pressure and societal norms are equally influential. According to respondents, friends were most frequently cited as the individuals who initiated or influenced their tobacco use. Additionally, a significant number mentioned common members of society as a factor in their initiation. Interestingly, while awareness about the health risks is high—86% agree that tobacco increases cancer risk and 89% agree that smoking kills—this awareness has not translated into strong societal resistance. In fact, 12.6% of respondents perceive smoking as fashionable, 22.4% are indifferent to their partner's tobacco use, and 31.8% view smoking as an easy way to socialize. Moreover, 17.2% of respondents find it difficult to refuse tobacco when offered by others, and 19.4% do not believe smoking is socially disapproved in public spaces.

These findings clearly illustrate that a pro-tobacco culture, peer pressure, and social acceptance continue to perpetuate tobacco use in Mizoram, despite rising health awareness. Additionally, the easy availability of tobacco products—including contraband items, as discussed in the previous chapter—further contributes to increased consumption.

5.2 Consumer Decision-Making and Tobacco Consumption

The Theory of Interpersonal Behaviour (Triandis, 1977) offers a valuable framework for understanding how personal beliefs, values, emotional responses, and social norms interact to shape an individual's consumption intentions and behaviours. In the context of Mizoram, this theoretical lens helps explain the factors that reinforce and sustain tobacco use, particularly among undergraduate students. Tobacco consumption among youth in the region appears to be influenced by a complex interplay of cognitive, emotional, and environmental cues that contribute to habit formation over time.

Primary data from the study indicates that the most frequently reported motivator for tobacco use is the conscious thought of personally possessing tobacco products, suggesting a strong internalised association with ownership and use. This is closely followed by the influence of observing others consume tobacco—indicating the power of social modelling and observational learning. Other prominent stimuli include the visual display of tobacco products in retail settings, portrayals of tobacco use in films and television shows, and the presence of tobacco-related advertisements. Notably, 28 percent of respondents stated that attractive packaging and brand names significantly enhanced their desire to smoke or use tobacco, highlighting the persuasive impact of branding and product aesthetics on youth consumption choices.

Beyond external triggers, internal attitudes and beliefs also play a crucial role. Nearly half (47.4%) of the respondents maintained that smoking or consuming tobacco is a matter of personal choice, one that should not be judged or interfered with by others. Meanwhile, 11 percent of students believed that tobacco use enhances their image, making them appear more mature or socially appealing. These beliefs and values collectively contribute to the formation of consumption intentions. When reinforced by favourable social settings—such as peer groups, communal behaviours, or perceived social acceptance—these intentions often translate into actual consumption behaviour. Over time, such behaviour may become habitual, driven by reinforcement mechanisms such as temporary emotional relief or social validation.

As discussed earlier in the book, the broader consumer behaviour and decision-making process in Mizoram is shaped by significant socio-cultural influences. These include familial patterns of tobacco use, peer pressure, prevailing societal attitudes, and the widespread availability and affordability of tobacco products. In addition, the study reveals patterns such as gender-based preferences, the tendency to choose low-cost alternatives, limited brand loyalty, and pro-tobacco mindsets. Situational triggers—such as stress, boredom, post-meal cravings or social gatherings—also play a critical role in influencing when and how students consume tobacco.

Moreover, the level of awareness about the harmful effects of tobacco and the expressed intentions to quit provide insight into the post-purchase evaluation phase of the decision-making process. While some students display an awareness of the health consequences and a desire to stop, this is often counterbalanced by the reinforcing social and psychological factors that sustain use. These findings offer important insights into the psychology of consumer decision-making and suggest valuable directions for intervention. Specifically, understanding these patterns can inform the design of targeted social marketing campaigns aimed at prevention and control of tobacco use among youth in Mizoram. Additionally, there is a strong case for extending such research to other states and regions to uncover regional variations and enable the development of more effective, context-sensitive strategies for tobacco control.

5.3 Integrating Civil Society and State Action for Effective Tobacco Control

The success of any tobacco control programme hinges on focused attention and coordinated efforts between government bodies and non-governmental organisations (NGOs) working closely with target populations. Since the late 20th century, global awareness of tobacco's detrimental effects on public health has grown significantly, prompting more organised interventions and stronger policy measures to curb tobacco consumption worldwide.

In 2003, the World Health Organisation (WHO) established the Framework Convention on Tobacco Control (WHO FCTC), which was adopted by 192 member states. India became a signatory to the treaty in 2004 and has since made comprehensive efforts to implement its provisions. A study revealed that following the implementation of the FCTC in India, smoking and smokeless tobacco use declined steeply by 52.9% and 17.6%, respectively. (Suliankatchi Abdulkader et al., 2019). Notably, even before joining the FCTC, India enacted a pioneering legislation in 2003: The Cigarettes and Other Tobacco Products (Prohibition of Advertisement and Regulation of Trade and Commerce, Production, Supply and Distribution) Act (COTPA). Further reinforcing these efforts, in 2007-08, the Ministry of Health and Family Welfare launched the National Tobacco Control Programme (NTCP) to enhance policy implementation and monitoring nationwide.

At the state level, Mizoram adopted the NTCP framework by establishing the Mizoram State Tobacco Control Programme (MSTCP) and the Mizoram State Tobacco Control Society (MSTCS), tasked with implementing the programme across the state. To ensure strict enforcement of tobacco laws, the Mizoram government has authorised police personnel at all ranks to enforce sections 4 and 6(a) & (b) of COTPA and has formed specialised Anti-Tobacco Squads (Hmar, 2018). Additional measures include enforcing smoking prohibitions in public places, especially government offices, and constituting a special committee to implement Article 5.3 of the WHO FCTC.

Since its inception, the MSTCS has spearheaded multiple initiatives such as the projects *Advocacy & Mobilisation for Smoke-Free Mizoram* and *Advancing Tobacco Control in Mizoram through Capacity Building and Strengthening Enforcement*. MSTCS operates Tobacco Control Cells statewide that provide treatment and counseling to individuals seeking to quit tobacco. Over time, MSTCS has successfully conducted anti-tobacco campaigns and mobilised key societal sectors—educational institutions, churches, and other NGOs—to join the tobacco control movement. For example, tobacco education has been integrated into school curricula, thematic sessions on tobacco and health have been introduced in church services, and community-level tobacco-free zones like Thingsul Tlangnuam have been adopted (Hatzaw, 2014).

Another key player in Mizoram's tobacco control landscape is the Indian Society on Tobacco and Health, Mizoram Chapter (ISTHMC). ISTHMC organised the first-ever World No Tobacco Day event in Mizoram, collaborating with the Tobacco Society of Mizoram and the Department of Health (Hatzaw, 2014). ISTHMC and MSTCS often partner in implementing tobacco control programmes, earning recognition and awards from WHO for their exemplary public-private advocacy and awareness efforts.

Beyond these specialised organisations, influential local NGOs such as the Young Mizo Association (YMA), Mizoram Hmeichhe Insuihkhawm Pawl (MHIP), Mizoram Zirlai Pawl (MZP), and Mizoram Journalist Association (MJA) have played vital roles in tobacco control initiatives. For instance, MHIP conducted a statewide campaign against Gutkha, while several YMA branches imposed bans on selling Gutkha in their respective localities (WebIndia123, 2010). The MJA, in collaboration with MSTCS and supported by The Union (an international voluntary scientific organization), organised a media workshop on tobacco control MZP also partnered with MSTCS to host the Youth MPOWER summit.

Religious organisations, particularly the churches, which have historically been vocal critics of alcoholism in Mizoram, remained largely silent for a long time on the issue of tobacco consumption (PahrüPou, 2017). However, some significant initiatives have since been undertaken. The Presbyterian Church, for instance, has adopted a policy of not recruiting probationary officers who are addicted to tobacco (Zorammuana, 2010). The Seventh-day Adventist Church holds a general stance against tobacco, deeming it "unclean" for human consumption. Additionally, the Presbyterian Church has incorporated a thematic focus on tobacco and health into its Wednesday night services (Hatzaw, 2014).

In conclusion, the sustained efforts of MSTCS and ISTHMC, supported by the broader Mizoram State Tobacco Control Programme, have yielded measurable progress. This is reflected in the decline of tobacco prevalence from 67.2% in the Global Adult Tobacco Survey (GATS) 2009-2010 to 58.7% in GATS 2016-2017. Nevertheless, this prevalence remains alarmingly high, underscoring the urgent need for intensified measures. Key challenges persist, including the widespread availability of contraband cigarettes, proximity of tobacco products to prohibited zones, and ongoing use of tobacco in public places.

On the positive side, Mizoram benefits from a strong network of non-governmental and religious organisations with substantial social influence, presenting a valuable opportunity to cultivate an anti-tobacco culture. However, the full potential of these organisations in tobacco control remains untapped and calls for deeper engagement and more strategic collaboration in the future.

5.4 Developing a Comprehensive and Integrated Approach for Tobacco Control

Lantz (2018) emphasizes that research on tobacco control programmes and policy initiatives has consistently demonstrated the need for a comprehensive approach. As recommended by the Centers for Disease Control and Prevention (CDC), such an approach should incorporate interventions targeting public knowledge and attitudes, increased costs through taxation, restrictions on youth access, reduction of environmental exposure, and robust cessation support. Similarly, Novotny and Mamudu (2008) define a comprehensive tobacco control programme as one that simultaneously works to shift social norms, enforce smoke-free policies, expand cessation services, and intensify efforts to prevent the initiation of tobacco use. This multi-faceted framework integrates educational, clinical, regulatory, economic, and social strategies.

To develop an effective and comprehensive tobacco control programme, it is crucial to integrate principles from the field of social marketing. Recognised as a promising intervention strategy, social marketing has demonstrated effectiveness across a variety of behaviours, target populations, and settings (Stead et al., 2007). However, the distinctive lifestyle, psychological makeup, and socio-economic and cultural context of Mizoram may limit the applicability of generalised social marketing strategies commonly used elsewhere. Drawing a parallel, Hu et al. (2013), in their study of the implementation barriers to the WHO Framework Convention on Tobacco Control (FCTC) in China, highlighted the importance of accounting for national specificities and advocated for a dual strategy combining top-down and bottom-up approaches. Similarly, in the context of Mizoram, a tailored yet comprehensive social marketing plan is required to effectively address the state's unique tobacco consumption dynamics.

To maximize the impact of tobacco control efforts in Mizoram, it is imperative to foster synergy among the various organisations engaged in this cause. The Mizoram State Tobacco Control Society (MSTCS), serving as the central nodal agency, is well-positioned to assume a leadership role in formulating a comprehensive social marketing strategy. This initiative should be supported by active collaboration with other stakeholders such as the Indian Society for Tobacco and Health, Mizoram Chapter (ISTHMC). An effective social marketing plan must be grounded in a well-structured marketing mix that identifies and integrates key strategic elements. According to Lee and Dewhirst (2011), the components of the social marketing mix—often referred to as the 4Ps—should be developed in a synergistic manner for optimal results. In the context of tobacco control in Mizoram, the adapted 4Ps framework[1]—Proposition, Perception, Platform, and Persuasion (Akhtar & Bhattacharjee, 2014)—offers a useful model for designing and implementing targeted interventions.

Singh and Ladusingh (2014) have advocated for a targeted, population-based approach to effectively control and reduce tobacco consumption in India. Similarly, Lee and Dewhirst (2011) categorize social marketing strategies for tobacco control into two primary types: prevention-focused and cessation-focused. To achieve sustainable reduction in tobacco prevalence in Mizoram, it is essential that social marketing efforts run parallel along both these

1. In 2014, the author presented a paper at the International Conference on Research in Marketing (ICRM 2013), held at IIT Delhi, which proposed a new set of marketing mix elements (4Ps) specifically tailored for Social Marketing.

approaches, guided by a segmentation strategy that distinguishes between current tobacco users and potential future users. The current tobacco consumers should be addressed through a curative approach, aimed at encouraging cessation, while prospective users should be targeted with preventive interventions to discourage initiation. The terms preventive and curative approaches are commonly associated with medicine and healthcare, and they also form a fundamental component of the World Health Organisation's definition of primary health care (WHO, 2019b). The following sections elaborate on how these two approaches can be applied in the context of social marketing for tobacco control in Mizoram.

(A) The Curative Approach

The curative approach in social marketing focuses on existing tobacco users, aiming to persuade them to quit. Several theoretical models can be applied to design effective interventions under this approach.

The Protection Motivation Theory (Rogers, 1975) is useful for understanding how individuals perceive health threats related to tobacco use and how these perceptions shape their intentions to quit or continue consumption. Primary data from the study indicates that 40.5% of the respondents among the ATC (Active Tobacco Consumers) acknowledge having health problems due to tobacco use, while 22.78% associate the word "harmful" with "tobacco." Furthermore, 82.1% of ATC respondents agree that tobacco increases the likelihood of developing cancer, and 87.66% believe that tobacco or smoking can be fatal. This perception is even stronger in the GATS 2 survey (MHFW, 2018), where 96.7% of adults recognised that both smoking and smokeless tobacco can lead to serious illnesses. These findings suggest a clear sense of *perceived vulnerability* among users—an important component in the threat appraisal process.

Social marketers must leverage this awareness to emphasize that quitting tobacco can significantly reduce or even prevent existing and future health complications. Additionally, 69.3% of ATC respondents perceive the monetary cost of tobacco consumption to be very high. This highlights the relevance of the Health Belief Model, which assesses perceived susceptibility, severity, benefits, and barriers to quitting. The model can guide efforts to motivate users to participate in tobacco cessation interventions by focusing on both health and economic incentives.

The Elaboration Likelihood Model (Petty & Cacioppo, 1983, 1986) is also applicable in crafting persuasive messages. It helps determine whether the target audience will engage in central or peripheral message processing. In conjunction, the Heuristic-Systematic Model (Chaiken, 1987) can be used to facilitate systematic processing of messages by ensuring that they are both logically compelling and emotionally resonant.

Campaign messages should also aim to induce Cognitive Dissonance (Festinger, 1957) in current tobacco users—creating discomfort when their consumption behaviour conflicts with their knowledge of its harms. Promoting non-consumption as a consistent and healthier alternative can help resolve this dissonance and encourage behaviour change.

Data from the primary study shows that 45.57% of ATC respondents intend to quit in the future, 32.28% are currently trying to quit, and 69.3% believe they can successfully quit tobacco. According to GATS 2 (TISS & MHFW, 2018), 53.5% of current smokers and 71.2% of smokeless tobacco users have either planned to or are contemplating quitting. These statistics suggest a strong motivational base, which can be further supported using the Theory of Trying (Bagozzi & Warshaw, 1990). This theory allows campaign designers to consider users' past behaviours, attitudes, and intentions while framing cessation strategies.

To effectively segment and target users, the Stages of Change Model (Prochaska & DiClemente, 1984, 1986) can be utilised. This model identifies six stages in the behavioural change process: Pre-contemplation, Contemplation, Preparation, Action, Maintenance, and Termination. Tailoring interventions to match the user's stage can significantly increase the likelihood of successful quitting.

As emphasized by Mohan and Lando (2016), tobacco cessation should be institutionalised as a paramedical discipline and integrated into primary healthcare services in Mizoram. Therefore, it may be essential to strengthen and expand the existing network of the State Tobacco Control Cell (STCC) and District Tobacco Control Cells (DTCCs) in Mizoram to further improve the effectiveness, accessibility, and outreach of tobacco control initiatives and cessation services. Additionally, the primary study reveals a significant association between gender and the type of tobacco products consumed. This points to the need for a gender-specific approach in tobacco control. For instance, targeted interventions for women who use smokeless tobacco could be particularly effective. Notably, Sweden's gender-specific tobacco control strategies led to a marked decrease in smoking rates among women (Patja et al., 2009).

(B) The Preventive Approach

The preventive approach focuses on creating a supportive social environment and fostering individual awareness to discourage and disapprove tobacco consumption among non-users and the general public in Mizoram. The aim is to instill and sustain a strong anti-tobacco attitude as a normative aspect of public behaviour.

In this context, the Theory of Reasoned Action (Fishbein & Ajzen, 1975) is a valuable framework to understand and predict individuals' intentions and prospective behaviours related to tobacco use. The theory examines how people develop beliefs—both personal and normative—about the consequences of consumption and non-consumption of tobacco, and how these beliefs influence their motivation to conform to perceived social expectations.

Findings from the primary study reveal that peer influence plays a significant role, with friends being the most common source of encouragement for tobacco use. Additionally, 83.5% of respondents among the Active Tobacco Consumers (ATC) reported having family members who also use tobacco. This suggests that family, friends, and broader societal norms can often act as enablers or tacit approvers of tobacco consumption—even for non-users.

Given this influence, there is an urgent need to raise awareness among families in Mizoram about the risks of tobacco use and their responsibility in shaping the health behaviour of younger generations. Social marketing interventions must therefore include de-normalisation campaigns (Lee & Dewhirst, 2011) aimed at challenging and transforming existing societal norms and the widespread acceptance of tobacco use.

Mass media should be strategically leveraged to disseminate anti-tobacco messages, while partnerships among governmental bodies, NGOs, educational institutions, and community organisations should be actively encouraged. A robust branding strategy for tobacco control is also essential to build a recognizable, relatable identity for the movement—helping to generate momentum and sustained public engagement.

From a policy and regulatory perspective, strict enforcement of the Cigarettes and Other Tobacco Products Act (COTPA), 2003 and its provisions in Mizoram is critical. This includes:

- Restricting the sale of contraband tobacco products
- Prohibiting the sale of tobacco to minors
- Enforcing bans on the sale of tobacco products in and around educational institutions
- Ensuring compliance with no-smoking regulations in public places

Moreover, alongside a blanket ban on tobacco advertising, authorities must remain vigilant about the innovative and manipulative marketing strategies employed by tobacco companies, which often aim to bypass regulations and appeal to younger first-time consumers.

Ultimately, a comprehensive preventive strategy requires the creation of a supportive socio-cultural and legal ecosystem—one that actively discourages tobacco use, reduces its social acceptability, and minimizes exposure to pro-tobacco influences across all segments of society.

5.5 Social Marketing Framework for Tobacco Control in Mizoram

The proposed Social Marketing Framework for Tobacco Control in Mizoram (Exhibit 5.1) integrates both curative and preventive approaches alongside the core components of the social marketing mix. This comprehensive framework is intended to guide strategic tobacco control efforts by addressing the needs of both current users and potential future consumers. The rationale for this framework is grounded in global evidence, which suggests that multi-component intervention strategies are particularly effective in reducing tobacco consumption, especially among youth (Flay, 2000; McAlister et al., 1979; Vartiainen et al., 1990). Mishra et al. (2005) also advocate for approaches that target the social, environmental, and intrapersonal factors influencing youth tobacco use. In alignment with these

Exhibit 5.1: Social Marketing Framework for Tobacco Control in Mizoram

WHO Framework Convention on Tobacco Control (WHO FCTC)

National Tobacco Control Programme (NTCP)

Mizoram State Tobbaco Control Programme (MSTCP)

MPOWER Measures | National Tobacco Control Programme (NTCP) | Mizoram State Tobbaco Control Programme (MSTCP)

Social Marketing Mix Strategy		
Marketing Mix Elements	Social Marketing Approach	
	Curative Approach	Preventive Approach
Proposition	➤ Communicate the advantages of quitting tobacco and offer 'quitting' as the only solution to negate harm caused by tobacco use. ➤ Set objectives for tobacco control. ➤ Communicate provisions of COTPA and ensure proper visibility of anti-tobacco signs/notifications in public places.	➤ Build awareness among the general population about the harms of tobacco use ➤ Seek public support and commitment for an ongoing anti-tobacco movement. ➤ Create branding for identification and popularization of the cause of tobacco control in Mizoram.
Perception	➤ Highlight the benefits of quitting over the cost of tobacco consumption.	➤ Deglamorize tobacco and smoking and promote the perception that smoking/tobacco is not cool.
Platform	➤ Identify segments among existing tobacco consumers and common public spaces like schools, colleges, offices etc. for tobacco control initiatives and interventions. ➤ Form quit-groups among the target tobacco consumers.	➤ Establish partnership with other organizations. ➤ Select media platforms for general promotion as well as interactive engagement of people to the cause of tobacco control.
Persuasion	➤ Apply relevant conceptual models related to communication, persuasion, attitude and behavior change to ensure quitting. ➤ Develop existing network and infrastructure of Tobacco Control Cells. ➤ Penalize offenders of COTPA	➤ Explore relevant conceptual models related to communication, persuasion and attitude change to alter "pro-tobacco" mindset and strengthen the "no-tobacco" mindset.

Mizoram State Tobbaco Control Programme (MSTCP) | National Tobacco Control Programme (NTCP) | MPOWER Measures

Mizoram State Tobbaco Control Programme (MSTCP)

National Tobacco Control Programme (NTCP)

WHO Framework Convention on Tobacco Control (WHO FCTC)

findings, the proposed framework calls for a comprehensive and integrated strategy rooted in the policy guidelines of the World Health Organisation Framework Convention on Tobacco Control (WHO FCTC), the MPOWER measures, the National Tobacco Control Programme (NTCP), and the Mizoram State Tobacco Control Programme (MSTCP). It is also important to highlight that the WHO FCTC provides a normative structure for global tobacco control (Reddy et al., 2010), while inputs from the Global Adult Tobacco Survey (GATS) offer critical data for tailoring national and state-level policies (Lal et al., 2015).

The Proposition strategy under the *curative approach* should focus on creating robust awareness among existing tobacco users about the harmful effects of tobacco consumption and position quitting as the only viable solution. Specific objectives must be defined, such as setting measurable targets for reducing overall tobacco use. Tailored communication content should be developed to promote quitting—preferably in the vernacular language—and should incorporate relatable non-verbal tools such as images and graphics to enhance message effectiveness. The provisions of the Cigarettes and Other Tobacco Products Act (COTPA), 2003, which outline various conditions and restrictions on the sale, purchase, and use of tobacco products, should be clearly communicated to the target audience. Additionally, the enforcement and visibility of Tobacco-Free (TF) policies—which have shown global efficacy in reducing both firsthand and secondhand smoke exposure (Ickes, 2017; Seitz, 2018)—must be ensured through prominent anti-tobacco signage in public spaces.

Under the *preventive approach*, the Proposition strategy should aim to build awareness among the general population—particularly the youth—about the dangers of tobacco use and garner their support and commitment for a sustained anti-tobacco movement. It is vital to educate non-smokers about the harms of passive smoking and to instill in them a strong sense of their right to a smoke-free environment (Hu et al., 2013). The strategy should also include focused branding efforts to identify, promote, and popularise the cause of tobacco control in Mizoram.

The Perception strategy for the *curative approach* should emphasize the tangible benefits of quitting tobacco, such as improved health and economic savings, over the continued costs and consequences of tobacco use. In contrast, the *preventive approach* should implement de-normalisation campaigns (Lee & Dewhirst, 2011) to challenge and dismantle the glamorised image of tobacco consumption, especially among youth, and promote the view that it is neither fashionable nor socially acceptable to smoke or consume tobacco.

The Platform strategy under the *curative approach* should begin by segmenting existing tobacco users—such as school and college students, office workers, and other at-risk groups—and identifying commonly frequented public spaces such as educational institutions and workplaces as sites for intervention. Initiatives like the formation of quit groups and cessation programmes tailored to these segments can be implemented effectively in these spaces. Conversely, the *preventive approach* should focus on establishing long-term partnerships with civil society organisations, non-governmental bodies, and key local associations such as the the YMA, churches, MZP, MHIP, and others. These partnerships can play a pivotal role in mobilizing community support and disseminating anti-tobacco messages at the grassroots level. Additionally, media platforms—such as local television channels, newspapers, sports events, and social media—should be strategically utilised for wide-reaching promotion and interactive public engagement. These platforms can help create sustained momentum for the anti-tobacco movement and reinforce the message across diverse segments of the population.

Finally, the Persuasion strategy for the *curative approach* should incorporate conceptual models of communication, persuasion, and behaviour change to motivate existing users to quit. Anti-tobacco campaigns should be guided by persuasive communication strategies to ensure they effectively influence attitudes, change behaviours, and encourage public support for tobacco control initiatives. Additionally, the approach should also focus on strengthening the infrastructure and network of Tobacco Control Cells and Cessation Clinics across the state and strictly enforcing penalties under COTPA, 2003, against violators. Meanwhile, the *preventive approach* should use similar behavioural and communication theories to transform societal attitudes, aiming to replace the prevailing "pro-tobacco" mindset with a resilient and widespread "no-tobacco" culture across Mizoram.

5.6 Roadmap to a Tobacco-Free Mizoram

A tobacco-free Mizoram demands a strategic roadmap with well-defined, context-sensitive, and actionable objectives. This section presents a set of integrated, evidence-backed recommendations designed to guide such a roadmap, grounded in the state's socio-cultural, economic, and behavioural realities. Building upon the insights presented in the preceding chapters and the proposed Social Marketing Framework for Tobacco Control in Mizoram (refer to Exhibit 5.1), this section outlines a series of strategic and actionable steps aimed at enhancing the overall effectiveness of tobacco control efforts in the state. These recommendations are structured to integrate community participation, behavioural change principles, enforcement mechanisms, effective interventions and health promotion strategies — all tailored to Mizoram's unique context.

The following measures are proposed to strengthen and sustain a tobacco-free movement across the state:

(A) Focus on Public Communication and Engagement:

A cornerstone of an effective tobacco control strategy in Mizoram is robust public communication and community engagement. There is a critical need to build widespread awareness among the general population about the health, economic, and social harms caused by tobacco use. This must be complemented with mass education and grassroots empowerment, aiming to mobilise individuals and communities to take collective action against tobacco consumption (Jandoo & Mehrotra, 2008; Jhanjee, 2011).

Strategic messaging should emphasize the benefits of quitting tobacco as the only viable solution to reverse or mitigate the harm caused by its use. Communication efforts must target current tobacco users, clearly highlighting how the benefits of quitting outweigh the perceived benefits or social appeal of consumption. Campaigns should focus on deglamourizing tobacco and dismantling the perception that smoking or chewing tobacco is "cool," thereby promoting a cultural shift in attitudes, particularly among the youth.

Special attention should also be paid to the hazards of second-hand smoke, with campaigns modeled on successful programmes such as California's Tobacco Control Program (CTCP) (Ekpu & Brown, 2015), which effectively communicated the dangers of passive smoking to families and communities.

To transform pro-tobacco attitudes and reinforce anti-tobacco mindsets, communication strategies must draw on established models of persuasion, attitude change, and behavioural communication. In this regard, the "de-normalisation" approach to tobacco control, as employed in Canada (Lee & Dewhirst, 2011), can be instrumental in portraying tobacco use as an undesirable social behaviour.

Innovative interventions such as retail point-of-sale guardianship (Gilbertson, 2007), which restricts youth access to tobacco products at the retail level, should be explored and implemented across urban and rural areas. Moreover, developing a cohesive branding strategy is essential to give a recognizable identity to the tobacco control movement in Mizoram. This includes the creation of compelling visuals, slogans, and narratives that resonate with Mizo values and youth culture.

Choosing the right communication platforms is equally critical. While traditional media (radio, television, newspapers) remains vital, digital platforms and social media offer interactive and scalable tools to reach younger demographics and foster community-level engagement (Freeman & Chapman, 2008; National Cancer Institute, 2008). In India, sustained mass media campaigns have already proven effective in changing attitudes and behaviours toward tobacco (Murukutla et al., 2012), and Mizoram can build on this momentum.

Importantly, Mizo society's strengths—such as a high literacy rate, strong community orientation, and respect for discipline and social order—can be leveraged to build a sustained, community-driven movement. By tapping into these positive social attributes, the state can cultivate a broad-based public consensus and grassroots ownership of the tobacco control agenda, ensuring its continuity and effectiveness in the long term.

(B) Ensuring Participation of Various Organisations:

Effective tobacco control in Mizoram requires the active involvement of a broad spectrum of organisations beyond just government agencies. Novotny and Mamudu (2008) observed that insufficient development of civil society hampers the effective implementation of the Framework Convention on Tobacco Control (FCTC), especially in low- and middle-income nations. This observation is highly relevant in the context of Mizoram, where civil society has a long-standing tradition of community engagement and social influence.

There is an urgent need for enhanced coordination and engagement among governmental, non-governmental, religious, and educational institutions to create a unified front against tobacco use (Reddy et al., 2012). In Mizoram, organisations such as the YMA, MHIP, MZP, and various Church bodies hold significant sway over public attitudes and community life. These entities should be proactively invited and encouraged to participate in the promotion of anti-tobacco culture and behaviour. Their involvement in awareness campaigns, cessation drives, and policy advocacy can amplify the reach and impact of government-led initiatives.

In addition to these influential NGOs and religious institutions, local self-government bodies such as village councils play a pivotal role in rural governance and community mobilisation. Their proximity to the grassroots, along with their credibility and administrative presence, positions them uniquely to implement tobacco control measures effectively. As Mohan et al. (2013) suggest, such institutions have the potential to influence both public opinion and policy discourse around tobacco control. Reddy and Gupta (2004) also recommend empowering village-level governance bodies to execute and monitor anti-tobacco programmes in rural areas, which can significantly enhance the effectiveness and sustainability of interventions.

Another vital domain for engagement is the education sector, Schools, colleges, and universities must be integrated into the tobacco control framework through curriculum design, awareness activities, and environmental strategies. Educational institutions should be encouraged to foster tobacco-free campuses, monitor and restrict tobacco use, and raise awareness among students, particularly targeting early intervention to prevent initiation during adolescence—a critical period when lifelong habits are often formed.

In summary, a multi-sectoral and multi-stakeholder approach is essential to build a comprehensive tobacco control ecosystem in Mizoram. Collaborative participation across organisations will help in mainstreaming anti-tobacco efforts, creating a sustained culture of prevention, and ensuring that tobacco control becomes a shared responsibility across all levels of society.

While institutional collaboration lays the foundation for a unified effort, legal enforcement ensures that this foundation is protected and strengthened.

(C) Strengthening the Existing Legal Environment

For effective tobacco control in Mizoram, it is essential to rigorously enforce the provisions of the Cigarettes and Other Tobacco Products Act (COTPA), 2003. As emphasized by several public health experts, including Dr. Jane Ralte (The Indian Express, May 27, 2010), strict implementation is critical to achieve the intended outcomes. Clear and visible anti-tobacco signage should be mandated at public places and points of sale. Moreover, the availability of tobacco products in and around educational institutions must be strictly prohibited, with regular and unannounced inspections to ensure compliance. Violations of COTPA provisions should be met with accountability and legal penalties as per the law.

Gupta (2006) observes that although the COTPA is sufficiently robust to meet most of the requirements outlined in the FCTC—and in some aspects even goes beyond the minimum standards—it still contains certain shortcomings that limit its overall effectiveness. One such significant challenge in Mizoram, as discussed earlier in

Chapter 4, is the widespread availability of contraband cigarettes. A report by Agarwal (2017) reveals that smuggled cigarettes from countries such as China, UAE, Indonesia, and Bangladesh constitute more than one-fifth of all cigarette sales in India. This issue is especially pronounced in Northeast India, given its close proximity to neighbouring countries, making it a hotspot for the influx of contraband cigarettes—which pose a significant threat to both public health and the region's economic sustainability (Agarwala & Barman, 2017).

In Mizoram, the low-end cigarette market is heavily infiltrated by illicit cigarettes, making young people especially vulnerable to tobacco use and nicotine addiction. This concern is further substantiated by the primary data collected in this study, which shows a significant number of users consuming contraband tobacco products.

Therefore, there is an urgent need to impose a complete ban on the sale and distribution of contraband cigarettes and tobacco products within Mizoram. Additionally, Mohan et al. (2018) highlight the potential of state-specific legislations in strengthening tobacco control. The Government of Mizoram should consider introducing a dedicated state law to address the unique challenges faced in the region, thereby supplementing the national framework with locally relevant and enforceable provisions.

(D) Making Effective and Accessible Interventions

The existing infrastructure and network of Tobacco Control Cells in Mizoram need to be strengthened, upgraded, and made more accessible, particularly for individuals residing in remote and rural areas. These facilities should serve not only as service delivery points but also as behavioural research hubs to generate contextually relevant cessation messages and strategies, as suggested by Nichter and Muramoto (2010). The community-pharmacist-based smoking cessation (CPSC) model—which has demonstrated success in countries like Thailand (Ekpu & Brown, 2015; Thavorn & Chaiyakunapruk, 2008)—may also be explored as a cost-effective and community-integrated intervention approach in Mizoram.

A segmentation approach should be adopted, identifying groups among current tobacco users based on their consumption patterns, socio-economic profiles, and motivational drivers. Tailored interventions and targeted cessation efforts, such as the formation of peer-supported "quit-groups," can be more effective when aligned with the specific needs and characteristics of these segments. Public platforms such as schools, colleges, workplaces, and community centers should be actively utilised to roll out awareness and cessation initiatives.

Additionally, incorporating relevant conceptual models from the fields of communication, persuasion, and behaviour change can significantly enhance the effectiveness of intervention campaigns by addressing the psychological and social dimensions of tobacco addiction. In rural areas where the infrastructure for formal cessation clinics may not be feasible in the short term, direct community-based interventions can serve as a practical alternative (Barik et al., 2016). These grassroots interventions should be centrally coordinated by the District Tobacco Control Cells, which must be equipped with sufficient resources, skilled personnel, and expanded capacity to oversee localised programme delivery and support.

(E) Controlling the Growing Trend of E-Cigarette Consumption

One of the emerging challenges in achieving a tobacco-free Mizoram is the rapid introduction and growing popularity of e-cigarettes and vaping devices in the state. These trends signify a notable shift in tobacco consumption patterns and require immediate and strategic attention. To effectively address this challenge, it is essential that future tobacco control initiatives in Mizoram expand their focus to include these new forms of nicotine delivery. This would involve not only regulatory measures but also preventive actions and awareness campaigns tailored to counter their rise and safeguard public health.

Despite the Prohibition of Electronic Cigarettes Act, 2019, which bans the sale and promotion of e-cigarettes and vaping devices in India, their use continues to grow, especially among the youth (Pettigrew et al., 2023). In May 2023, the Ministry of Health, Government of India, issued notices to 15 websites selling e-cigarettes, directing them to cease the advertisement and sale of such products (The Economic Times, October 2, 2023).

Exhibit 5.2: Sale of E-Cigarettes on Social Media in Mizoram

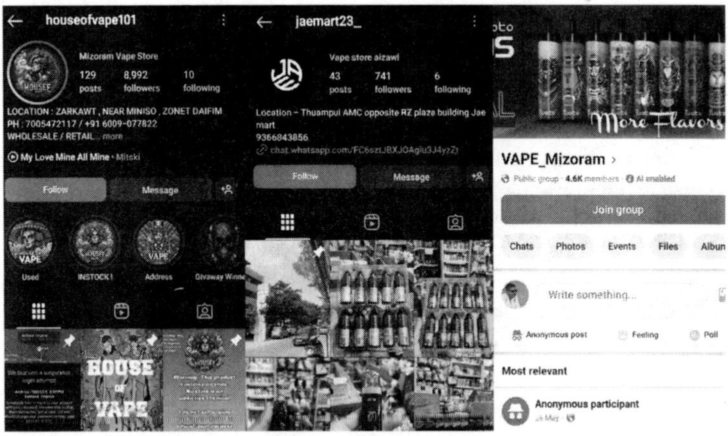

In Mizoram, e-cigarettes and vaping devices are easily accessible, with many sellers utilising popular social media platforms such as Instagram, Facebook, and WhatsApp to market and sell these products. Exhibit 5.2 shows the online availability of e-cigarettes and vapes in Mizoram, highlighting the extent of this issue. Therefore, there is an urgent need for stricter enforcement of all provisions of the Prohibition of Electronic Cigarettes Act, 2019, In particular, greater attention must be given to controlling the sale of e-cigarettes through online platforms.

(F) Monitoring, Feedback and Control

Lee and Dewhirst (2011) underscore the importance of ongoing evaluation, stating that social marketing campaigns must be assessed on a continuous basis. This principle holds critical importance for tobacco control efforts in Mizoram. A comprehensive mechanism for monitoring, feedback, and control must be developed and integrated into all phases of planning, execution, and evaluation of tobacco control strategies. Such a system should facilitate regular assessment of the current status of tobacco consumption, track progress made through implemented interventions, and ensure strategic flexibility and adaptive decision-making. Robust control mechanisms will also help maintain the integrity and effectiveness of ongoing initiatives.

The latest data from the Global Adult Tobacco Survey (GATS) should be actively utilised to inform the monitoring process and shape evidence-based policies. An upstream social marketing approach is equally essential—focusing not only on consumer behaviour but also on influencing policy and regulatory frameworks that govern the tobacco industry. One significant policy recommendation in this regard is the implementation of plain packaging for tobacco products.

Plain packaging refers to the standardisation of packaging design, removing all brand-specific logos, colours, and promotional elements, with only the brand name displayed in a standardized font, typeface, and position (Moodie et al., 2011). This aligns with the World Health Organisation's FCTC guidelines under Article 13, which advocate for the elimination of any form of advertising or promotion on tobacco packaging, including individual units (WHO, 2008b; WHO, 2016). Attractive packaging is one of the most powerful tools the tobacco industry uses to promote consumption and brand loyalty (WHO, 2016), particularly among youth and new users.

Primary data from the field study indicates a significant correlation between visually appealing tobacco packaging and increased desire to consume tobacco products. In light of this, Jhanjee (2011) has advocated for the enforcement of generic (plain) tobacco packaging in India to diminish the allure of tobacco products. International evidence strongly supports this measure. For instance, studies from Australia have shown that plain packaging significantly reduces the attractiveness, promotional value, and social appeal of tobacco products while enhancing the visibility and impact of health warnings (Australia India Institute, 2012; Moodie et al., 2012; WHO, 2016).

The Australia India Institute Taskforce on Tobacco Control (2012) concluded that plain packaging could prevent experimentation and initiation among children and youth, support cessation efforts, and reduce overall consumption. Therefore, implementing plain packaging in Mizoram could serve as a powerful tool to reduce the visibility and appeal of tobacco products, especially among young and vulnerable populations.

Exhibit 5.3: A Visual Guide for Plain Packaging

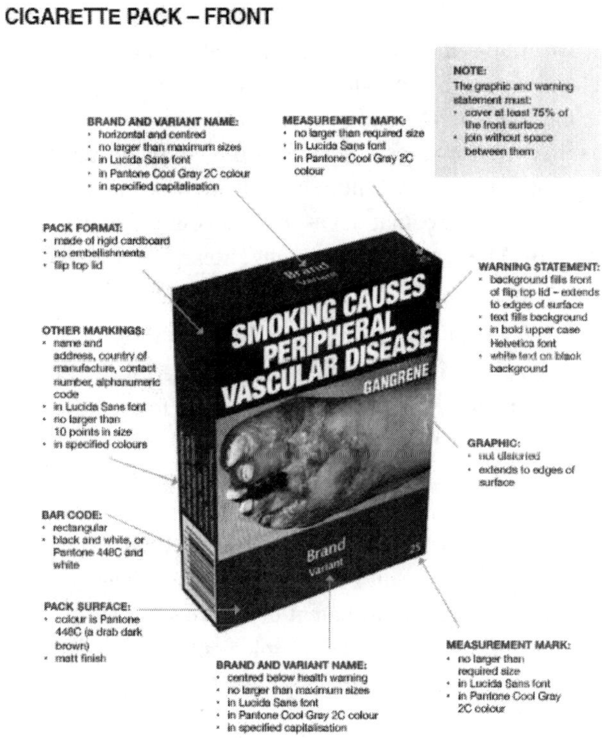

Source: Department of Health, Australian Government (2018).

The exhibit 5.3 illustrates the standardised design features of plain cigarette packaging as implemented by the Australian Government. The Australian experience, along with the comprehensive findings of the Australia India Institute Taskforce, offers a valuable roadmap for evaluating, planning, and executing plain packaging policies in the Indian context, including Mizoram. These insights can significantly contribute to shaping a more effective and impactful tobacco control policy framework.

* * * *

Mohan et al. (2018) emphasize the value of culture-based strategies for enhancing the effectiveness of tobacco control policies. In the context of Mizoram, where tobacco use is deeply influenced by unique socio-cultural, psychological, and economic factors, it is imperative to delve into the underlying causes and motivations behind such addictive behaviours. Generic social marketing and intervention models that prove effective elsewhere may not yield the same results in Mizoram unless they are tailored to the local context. Therefore, a comprehensive, culturally sensitive social marketing strategy is essential—one that takes into account the distinctive characteristics of Mizo society, including lifestyle, attitudes, and community values.

The proposed social marketing framework in this book offers a structured and locally adaptable approach to guide tobacco control efforts in Mizoram, providing valuable direction for policymakers and stakeholders. To enhance the effectiveness of tobacco control in the state, several key measures are recommended: a strong emphasis on public communication and engagement to raise awareness and shift attitudes; active participation from diverse civil society and community organisations to build widespread support; reinforcement and expansion of the legal environment to ensure strict enforcement and address emerging challenges; implementation of effective and accessible intervention strategies tailored to local needs; and the establishment of robust monitoring, feedback, and control mechanisms to continuously evaluate progress and adapt strategies as necessary.

In conclusion, the road to a tobacco-free Mizoram lies in balancing what we know works—community-based action, strong legal enforcement, and strategic communication—with the ability to swiftly respond to emerging challenges like e-cigarettes. As Allan Brandt aptly noted, the future of tobacco control rests in applying proven strategies while staying agile in the face of changing cultures and technologies (Zatoński & Stokłosa, 2017). For Mizoram, this means crafting a dynamic, inclusive, and culturally-rooted tobacco control movement—one that transforms public consciousness and protects future generations.

References

Agaku, I. T., Ayo-Yusuf, O. A., Vardavas, C. I., Alpert, H. R., & Connolly, G. N. (2013). Use of conventional and novel smokeless tobacco products among U.S. adolescents. *Pediatrics, 132*(3), e578–e586. https://doi.org/10.1542/peds.2013-0843

Agaku, I. T., & Ayo-Yusuf, O. A. (2014). The effect of exposure to pro-tobacco advertising on experimentation with emerging tobacco products among U.S. adolescents. *Health Education & Behavior, 41*(3), 275–280. https://doi.org/10.1177/1090198113511817

Agarwal, S. (2017, January 16). High taxes leading to rise in sale of smuggled cigarettes, says tobacco body. *Mint.* https://www.livemint.com/Politics/dV7uWd66ng41IVyacvC0VJ/High-taxes-leading-to-rise-in-sale-of-smuggled-cigarettes-s.html

Agarwala, D., & Barman, A. (2017, October 10–11). *Existence of contraband cigarettes in North East India: A study on socio-legal issues for human health and sustainability* [Conference paper]. 1st National Conference on Think Global Act Local: Contemporary Sustainable Business Practice and Development, NEMA & UNTM, Meghalaya, India.

Ahmed, F. M. A., & Peeran, S. W. (2016). Significance and determinants of tobacco use: A brief review. *Dentistry and Medical Research, 4*(2), 33–38. https://doi.org/10.4103/2348-1471.184726

Akhtar, S., & Bhattacharjee, M. (2014, December 21–22). *Marketing mix elements of social cause marketing: A rational approach to derive the new 4Ps* [Conference paper]. International Conference for Research in Marketing (ICRM 2013), IIT Delhi, XLRI Jamshedpur, and Curtin University, Australia.

Alonso, H. (1988). *Diversification in the cigarette industry in the 1980's* (Master's thesis). University of Richmond. https://scholarship.richmond.edu/masters-theses/1308

Ankathil, R. (2010). Tobacco, genetic susceptibility and lung cancer. *Tobacco Use Insights, 3*, 1–15. https://doi.org/10.4137/TUI.S4461

Arora, M., Gupta, V. K., Nazar, P. G., Stigler, M. H., Perry, C. L., & Reddy, K. S. (2012a). Impact of tobacco advertisements on tobacco use among urban adolescents in India: Results from a longitudinal study. *Tobacco Control, 21*(3), 318–324. https://doi.org/10.1136/tobaccocontrol-2011-050040

Arora, M., Mathur, N., Gupta, V. K., Nazar, P. G., Reddy, K. S., & James, S. D. (2012b). Tobacco use in Bollywood movies: Tobacco promotion activities and their association with tobacco use among Indian adolescents. *Tobacco Control, 21*(5), 482–487. https://doi.org/10.1136/tobaccocontrol-2011-050136

Arowolo, O. (2015). Uses and gratification theory and tobacco advertising necessity: An exposé. *International Journal of Broadcasting and Communication Technology, 3*(1), 81–98.

Australia India Institute. (2012). *Report of the Australia-India Institute Taskforce on Tobacco Control*. Australia India Institute, Australian Government Department of Industry, Innovation, Science, Research and Tertiary Education. https://www.indiaatmelbourne.unimelb.edu.au/publications/tobacco-control-report

Bagozzi, R. P., & Warshaw, P. R. (1990). Trying to consume. *Journal of Consumer Research, 17*(2), 127–140. https://doi.org/10.1086/208543

Baker, E. H. (2014). Socioeconomic status, definition. In A. C. Michalos (Ed.), *Encyclopedia of quality of life and well-being research*. Springer. https://onlinelibrary.wiley.com/doi/full/10.1002/9781118410868.wbehibs395

Bandura, A. (1977). *Social learning theory*. Prentice-Hall.

Barik, A., Rai, R. K., Gorain, A., Majumdar, S., & Chowdhury, A. (2016). Socio-economic disparities in tobacco consumption in rural India: Evidence from a health and demographic surveillance system. *Perspectives in Public Health, 136*(5), 278–287. https://doi.org/10.1177/1757913915609947

Bartal, M. (2001). Health effects of tobacco use and exposure. *Monaldi Archives for Chest Disease, 56*(6), 545–555.

Bhonde, P. (2016, December 4). Cancer cases on the rise in Mizoram, state being called 'Cancer Capital of India'. *IndiaTimes*. https://www.indiatimes.com/news/india/cancer-cases-on-the-rise-in-mizoram-state-being-called-cancer-capital-ofindia-263190.html

Bhonsle, R. B., Murti, P. R., & Gupta, P. C. (1992). *Tobacco habits in India*. Oxford University Press.

Biener, L., & Hargraves, J. L. (2014). A longitudinal study of electronic cigarette use among a population-based sample of adult smokers: Association with smoking cessation and motivation to quit. *Nicotine & Tobacco Research, 17*(2), 127–133. https://doi.org/10.1093/ntr/ntu200

Borio, G. (2001). *The tobacco timeline*. Retrieved July 6, 2019, from http://grace4life.com/History_of_Tobacco-by_Gene_Borio.pdf

Brandt, A. M. (2007). *The cigarette century: The rise, fall, and deadly persistence of the product that defined America*. Basic Books.

Brown, A., & Moodie, C. (2009). The influence of tobacco marketing on adolescent smoking interventions via normative beliefs. *Health Education Research, 24*(5), 721–733. https://doi.org/10.1093/her/cyp013

Business Dictionary. (2019). Definition, socioeconomic. WebFinance Inc. http://www.businessdictionary.com/definition/socioeconomic.html

Business Wire. (2019, March 20). The tobacco market in India (2018–2023): Leading players are ITC, Kothari Products, Godfrey Phillips India, VST Industries, Golden Tobacco Company, and NTC Industries. https://www.businesswire.com/news/home/20190320005593/en/Tobacco-Market-India-2018-2023-Leading-Players-ITC

Carter, O. B., Mills, B. W., & Donovan, R. J. (2009). The effect of retail cigarette pack displays on unplanned purchases: Results from immediate postpurchase interviews. *Tobacco Control, 18*(3), 218–221. https://doi.org/10.1136/tc.2008.027870

Chadda, R. K., & Sengupta, S. N. (2002). Tobacco use by Indian adolescents. *Tobacco Induced Diseases, 1*(2), 111–119. https://doi.org/10.1186/1617-9625-1-2-111

Chaiken, S. (1987). Heuristic versus systematic information processing and the use of source versus message cues in persuasion. *Journal of Personality and Social Psychology, 45*(4), 805–818. https://doi.org/10.1037/0022-3514.45.4.805

Chakraborty, A. S. (2017, August 23–25). *Social imaginaries and medical dystopia: 'Health migrations and care-givers' in Kolkata city from Mizoram* [Conference paper]. Sixth Critical Studies Conference: Refugees, Migrants, Violence and the Transformation of Cities, Mahanirban Calcutta Research Group (MCRG), Kolkata. http://www.mcrg.ac.in/6thCSC/6thCSC_Full_Papers/Anup.pdf

Charlton, A. (2004). Medicinal uses of tobacco in history. *Journal of the Royal Society of Medicine, 97*(6), 292–296. https://doi.org/10.1258/jrsm.97.6.292

Chattopadhyayya, A. (2000). Emperor Akbar as a healer and his eminent physicians. *Bulletin of Indian Institute of History of Medicine, 30*, 15–18.

Chaudhary, K. (2001). *Prevalence of tobacco use in Karnataka and Uttar Pradesh in India*. All India Institute of Medical Sciences (AIIMS) & Indian Council of Medical Research (ICMR).

Chawngthanmawii. (2014). *Role of NGOs in Mizoram with special reference to Young Mizo Association* (Post-Doctoral thesis, University of Madras). Shodhganga. http://hdl.handle.net/10603/203599

Chikkala, K. K. (2014). Tobacco marketing in South India and global impact on local labour relations. *South Asia Research, 34*(1), 47–64. https://doi.org/10.1177/0262728013517029

Choi, J., Payne, T. J., Ma, J. Z., & Ming, D. (2017). Relationship between personality traits and nicotine dependence in male and female smokers of African-American and European-American samples. *Frontiers in Psychiatry, 8*, 122. https://doi.org/10.3389/fpsyt.2017.00122

Clarance, D. (2025, May 31). *From trend to trap: The silent vaping crisis gripping India's teenagers*. *India Today*. Retrieved June 2, 2025, from https://www.indiatoday.in/health/story/teen-vaping-rises-india-cigarette-decline-nicotine-harm-legal-gaps-2733399-2025-05-31

Code of Federal Regulations. (2018). Title 21, Volume 8, Revised as of April 1, 2018 [CITE: 21CFR1100]. https://www.accessdata.fda.gov/scripts/cdrh/cfdocs/cfcfr/CFRSearch.cfm?CFRPart=1100&showFR=1

Consumer Advocates for Smoke-free Alternatives Association. (n.d.). *A historical timeline of electronic cigarettes*. Retrieved July 27, 2019, from http://www.casaa.org/historical-timeline-of-electronic-cigarettes/

Crawford, J. (1853). On the history and consumption of tobacco. *Journal of the Statistical Society of London, 16*(1), 45–52. https://doi.org/10.2307/2338282

Cussen, A., & McCool, J. (2011). Tobacco promotion in the Pacific: The current state of tobacco promotion bans and options for accelerating progress. *Asia-Pacific Journal of Public Health, 23*(1), 70–78. https://doi.org/10.1177/1010539510390925

Department of Economics & Statistics. (n.d.). *Top 10 killer diseases (2006)*. Government of Mizoram. Retrieved September 3, 2014, from http://desmizo.nic.in/Diseases.htm

Department of Health, Australian Government. (2018, April 26). *Tobacco plain packaging—Your guide*. https://www1.health.gov.au/internet/main/publishing.nsf/Content/tppbook#top

Directorate of Economics & Statistics. (2018). *Statistical abstract of Mizoram: 2017*. Government of Mizoram.

Do, E. K., Green, T. L., Prom-Wormley, C., & Fuemmeler, B. F. (2018). Social determinants of smoke exposure during pregnancy: Findings from waves 1 & 2 of the Population Assessment of Tobacco and Health (PATH) study. *Preventive Medicine Reports, 12*, 312–320. https://doi.org/10.1016/j.pmedr.2018.10.020

Donovan, R., & Henley, N. (2010). *Principles and practices of social marketing: An international perspective* (pp. 102–110, 125–156, 263–267, 284–285). Cambridge University Press.

Dube, S. R., Arrazola, R. A., Lee, J., Engstrom, M., & Malarcher, A. (2013). Pro-tobacco influences and susceptibility to smoking cigarettes among middle and high school students—United States, 2011. *Journal of Adolescent Health, 52*(Suppl. 5), S45–S51. https://doi.org/10.1016/j.jadohealth.2012.07.00

Dutra, L. M., & Glantz, S. A. (2014). Electronic cigarettes and conventional cigarette use among US adolescents: A cross-sectional study. *JAMA Pediatrics, 168*, 610–617. https://doi.org/10.1001/jamapediatrics.2013.5488

Dutt, A. (2018, May 30). Northeastern states have highest prevalence of tobacco use, says report. *Hindustan Times*. https://www.hindustantimes.com/health/northeastern-states-have-highest-prevalence-of-tobacco-use-says-report/story-Lb1C4W20vb1RGM1dGpCLDL.html

Efroymson, D., Pham, H. A., Jones, L., FitzGerald, S., Thu le, T., & Hien le, T. T. (2011). Tobacco and poverty: Evidence from Vietnam. *Tobacco Control, 20*(4), 296–301. https://doi.org/10.1136/tc.2010.039735

Ekpu, V. U., & Brown, A. K. (2015). The economic impact of smoking and of reducing smoking prevalence: Review of evidence. *Tobacco Use Insights, 8*, 1–35. https://doi.org/10.4137/TUI.S15628

Engel, J. F., Kollat, D. T., & Blackwell, R. D. (1968). *Consumer behaviour*. Holt, Rinehart & Winston.

Eriksen, M., Mackay, J., & Ross, H. (2012). *The tobacco atlas* (4th ed.). American Cancer Society.

Eriksen, M., Mackay, J., Schulger, N., Gomeshtaphe, F. I., & Drope, J. (2015). *The tobacco atlas* (5th ed.). American Cancer Society.

Esson, K. M., & Leeder, S. R. (2004). *The millennium development goals and tobacco control: An opportunity for global partnership*. World Health Organization.

Evans, N., Farkas, A., Gilpin, E., Berry, C., & Pierce, J. P. (1995). Influence of tobacco marketing and exposure to smokers on adolescent susceptibility to smoking. *Journal of the National Cancer Institute, 87*(20), 1538–1545. https://doi.org/10.1093/jnci/87.20.1538

Eysenck, H., Tarrant, M., Woolf, M., & England, L. (1960). Smoking and personality. *The British Medical Journal, 1*(5184), 1456–1460. https://doi.org/10.1136/bmj.1.5184.1456

Feighery, E. C., Henriksen, L., Wang, Y., Schleicher, N. C., & Fortmann, S. P. (2006). An evaluation of four measures of adolescents' exposure to cigarette marketing in stores. *Nicotine & Tobacco Research, 8*, 751–759. https://doi.org/10.1080/14622200601004125

Festinger, L. (1957). *A theory of cognitive dissonance*. Stanford University Press.

Financial Express. (2018, March 25). Was cheated into doing Pan Bahar ad, Pierce Brosnan tells Indian authorities. *Financial Express*. https://www.financialexpress.com/entertainment/was-cheated-into-doing-pan-bahar-ad-pierce-brosnan-tells-indian-authorities/1099462/

Fishbein, M., & Ajzen, I. (1975). *Belief, attitude, intention and behaviour: An introduction to theory and research*. Addison-Wesley.

Flay, B. R. (2000). Approaches to substance use prevention utilizing school curriculum plus social environment change. *Addictive Behaviors, 12*(6), 861–885.

Fouad, H., Awa, F. E., Naga, R. A. E., Emam, A. H., Labib, S., Palipudi, K. M., … Talley, B. (2016). Prevalence of tobacco use among adults in Egypt, 2009. *Global Health Promotion, 23*(2), 38–47. https://doi.org/10.1177/1757975913499801

Foulds, J., Ramstrom, L., Burke, M., & Fagerström, K. (2003). Effect of smokeless tobacco (snus) on smoking and public health in Sweden. *Tobacco Control, 12*, 349–359. https://doi.org/10.1136/tc.12.4.349

Freeman, B., & Chapman, S. (2008). Gone viral? Heard the buzz? A guide for public health practitioners and researchers on how Web 2.0 can subvert advertising restrictions and spread health information. *Journal of Epidemiology & Community Health, 62*(9), 778–782. https://doi.org/10.1136/jech.2008.077032

Freeman, B., & Chapman, S. (2010). British American Tobacco on Facebook: Undermining Article 13 of the global World Health Organisation Framework Convention on Tobacco Control. *Tobacco Control, 19*(3), e1–e9. https://doi.org/10.1136/tc.2009.032847

Gately, I. (2001). *Tobacco: A cultural history of how an exotic plant seduced civilization*. Simon & Schuster, 10, 22, 38.

Ghany, H. A. A. (2006). The association between indoor radon and tobacco smoke. *Indoor and Built Environment, 15*(3), 289–293. https://doi.org/10.1177/1420326X06066335

Gilbertson, T. (2007). Retail point-of-sale guardianship and juvenile tobacco purchases: Assessing the prevention capabilities of undergraduate college students. *Journal of Drug Education, 37*(1), 1–30.

Glanz, K., & Bishop, D. B. (2010). The role of behavioural science theory in development and implementation of public health interventions. *Annual Review of Public Health, 31*, 399–418. https://doi.org/10.1146/annurev.publhealth.012809.103604

Goniewicz, M. L., Knysak, J., Gawron, M., Kosmider, L., Sobczak, A., Kurek, J., ... Havel, C. (2014). Levels of selected carcinogens and toxicants in vapour from electronic cigarettes. *Tobacco Control, 23*, 133–139. https://doi.org/10.1136/tobaccocontrol-2012-050859

Gordon, D., Smith, G. D., Kelly, M., Subramanian, S. V., & Nandy, S. (2004). Health behaviour in context. *Economic and Political Weekly, 39*(7), 579–581.

Grana, R., Benowitz, N., & Glantz, S. A. (2014). E-cigarettes: A scientific review. *Circulation, 129*(19), 1972–1986. https://doi.org/10.1161/CIRCULATIONAHA.114.007667

Gupta, P. C. (2006). Tobacco control in India. *Indian Journal of Medical Research, 123*, 579–582. https://www.researchgate.net/publication/6912399_Tobacco_control_in_India

Gupta, P. C., & Ray, C. S. (2004a). Epidemiology of betel quid usage. *Annals of the Academy of Medicine, 33*(4 Suppl), 31–36.

Gupta, P. C., & Ray, C. S. (2004b). Tobacco epidemic in India. In *Science, policy and public health* (Vol. 44, pp. 253–266).

Hanghal, N. (2014, June 18). *Meet the woman who has been leading Mizo women's push for legal reforms for 40 years*. The Better India. https://www.thebetterindia.com/11629/mizo-women-for-legal-reforms-empowerment-pi-sangkhumi/

Hastings, G., & Saren, M. (2003). The critical contribution of social marketing: Theory and application. *Marketing Theory, 3*(3), 305–321.

Hatzaw, E. (2014). *Psychosocial aspects of tobacco use among Mizo women* (Doctoral dissertation). Department of Social Work, School of Social Sciences, Mizoram University, Aizawl.

Hatzaw, E. (2015). Self-reported perceptions on tobacco-related health consequences among women tobacco users. *International Journal of Research in Economics and Social Sciences, 5*(3), 83–94.

Hawkins, D. I., Best, R. J., Coney, K. A., & Mookerjee, A. (2007). *Consumer behaviour: Building marketing strategy* (9th ed.). Tata McGraw-Hill.

Hawkins, D. I., Motherbaugh, D. L., & Mookerjee, A. (2010). *Consumer behaviour: Building marketing strategy* (11th ed.). Tata McGraw-Hill. ISBN-13: 978-0-07-068216-0; ISBN-10: 0-07-068216-X

Health & Family Welfare Department. (2018). *Tobacco*. Government of Mizoram. https://health.mizoram.gov.in/page/tobacco

HealthHub. (2018). *Questions on smoking, tobacco use and health*. Ministry of Health, Singapore. https://www.healthhub.sg/live-healthy/597/questions_smoking

Henningfield, J. E., Fant, R. V., & Tomar, S. L. (1997). Smokeless tobacco: An addicting drug. *Advances in Dental Research, 11*(3), 330–335.

Henriksen, L., Schleicher, N. C., Feighery, E. C., & Fortmann, S. P. (2010). A longitudinal study of exposure to retail cigarette advertising and smoking initiation. *Pediatrics, 126*, 232–238. https://doi.org/10.1542/peds.2009-3021

Hindustan Times. (2003, October 13). *History of Mizoram*. https://www.hindustantimes.com/india/history-of-mizoram/story-eyhdTkw7geVDRHAgA4BBsN.html

Hmar, S. (2018, September 12). State Anti-Tobacco Day: Two villages in Mizoram declared 'smoke-free'. *Northeast Now*. Retrieved May 17, 2020, https://nenow.in/north-east-news/state-anti-tobacco-day-two-villages-in-mizoram-declared-smoke-free.html

Hofstetter, C. R., Ayers, J. W., Irvin, V. L., Sim, D. E. K., Hughes, S. C., Reighard, F., & Hovell, M. F. (2010). Does church participation facilitate tobacco control? A report on Korean immigrants. *Journal of Immigrant and Minority Health, 12*(2), 187–197. https://doi.org/10.1007/s10903-009-9228-9

Holmes, G. K. (1923). Some features of tobacco history. *Agricultural History Society Papers, 2*, 385, 387–407.

Hoof, L. V. (2011). *Tobacco (Nicotiana tabacum)*. http://bioweb.uwlax.edu/bio203/2011/vanhoof_loga/classification.htm

Hoyer, W. D., MacInnis, D. J., & Pieters, R. (2013). *Consumer behaviour* (6th ed.). South Western, Cengage Learning.

Hu, T., Lee, A. H., & Mao, Z. (2013). WHO Framework Convention on Tobacco Control in China: Barriers, challenges and recommendations. *Global Health Promotion, 20*(4), 13–22. https://doi.org/10.1177/1757975913501910

Hueiyen News Service. (2014, July 6). Role of Mizo women lauded. *Newmai News Network*. http://e-pao.net/GP.asp?src=34..070714.jul14

Hussain, A. (2008). Understanding the dynamics of tobacco consumption and control: A global perspective. In A. Hussain & N. Karamakar (Eds.), *Tobacco consumption: Socio-economic implications* (pp. 2–13). The ICFAI University Press. ISBN: 81-314-1397-7

Ickes, M. J., Rayens, M. K., Wiggins, A., & Hahn, E. J. (2017). Students' beliefs about and perceived effectiveness of a tobacco-free campus policy. *Policy, Politics, & Nursing Practice, 18*(1), 17–25. https://doi.org/10.1177/1527154417700633

India Brand Equity Foundation. (2019). *Industrial development & economic growth in Mizoram, March 2019*. Ministry of Commerce & Industry, Government of India. https://www.ibef.org/states/mizoram-presentation

India Brand Equity Foundation. (2023). *Mizoram*. Ministry of Commerce & Industry, Government of India. https://www.ibef.org/states/mizoram

India Brand Equity Foundation. (2024). *Mizoram*. Ministry of Commerce & Industry, Government of India. https://www.ibef.org/states/mizoram

Indian NGOs. (n.d.). *Mizo Hmeichhe Insuihkhawm Pawl*. Retrieved May 19, 2019, from http://www.indianngos.org/ngo_detail.aspx?nprof=246392243

International Institute for Population Sciences. (2010). *Global Adult Tobacco Survey (GATS) fact sheet India 2009–2010*. https://www.who.int/tobacco/surveillance/en_tfi_india_gats_fact_sheet.pdf

International Institute for Population Sciences. (2025). *Request for proposal for conducting GATS-3 fieldwork*. Ministry of Health and Family Welfare, Government of India. https://www.iipsindia.ac.in/sites/default/files/Grp-5-GATS-3%20RFP%20WB%26ADN_22%20Jan%202025.pdf

Jamal, A., Park-Lee, E., Birdsey, J., et al. (2024). Tobacco product use among middle and high school students — National Youth Tobacco Survey, United States. *MMWR Morbidity and Mortality Weekly Report, 73*(41), 917–924.

Jandoo, T., & Mehrotra, R. (2008). Tobacco control in India: Present scenario and challenges ahead. *Asian Pacific Journal of Cancer Prevention, 9*, 805–810.

Jatoi, I., Cummings, K. M., & Cazap, E. (2009). Global tobacco problem getting worse, not better. *Journal of Oncology Practice, 5*(1). https://ascopubs.org/doi/full/10.1200/JOP.0918501

Jenner, A. (2014). America's first cash crop: Tobacco. *Modern Farmer.* Retrieved July 06, 2019, from https://modernfarmer.com/2014/05/americas-first-cash-crop-tobacco/

Jhanjee, S. (2011). Tobacco control in India—Where are we now? *Delhi Psychiatry Journal, 14*(1), 26–32.

Jindal, S. K., Aggarwal, A. N., Gupta, D., Kashyap, S., & Chaudhary, D. (2005). Prevalence of tobacco use among school-going youth in North Indian states. *Indian Journal of Chest Diseases and Allied Sciences, 47*, 161–166.

John, R. M. (2005). Tobacco consumption patterns and its health implications in India. *Health Policy, 71*(2), 213–222.

John, R. M., Rao, R. K., Rao, M. G., Moore, J., Deshpande, R. S., Sengupta, J., … Jha, P. (2010). *The economics of tobacco taxation in India*. International Union Against Tuberculosis and Lung Disease (The Union). ISBN: 978-2-914365-70-3

Kalra, A. (2017, July 22). Govt to quiz Philip Morris on marketing of Marlboro cigarettes in India. *Reuters*. https://www.livemint.com/Companies/zKOQ7bg5sDxFgFbiIhXwpL/Govt-to-quiz-Philip-Morris-on-marketing-of-Marlboro-in-India.html

Kalra, A., Bansal, P., Lasseter, T., & Wilson, D. (2017). Cigarette companies woo young people in India while health officials are fuming. *Mint*. https://www.livemint.com/Companies/SuGHIYuzGX9ZvD0YZL9XrN/Cigarette-companies-woo-young-people-in-India-while-health-o.html

Kangla Online. (2016, November 24). Mizoram, the highest tobacco consuming state in the whole world. *Kangla Online*. http://kanglaonline.com/2016/11/mizoram-the-highest-tobacco-consuming-state-in-the-whole-world/

Karmakar, S. (2018, December 4). Mizoram: Chinese cigarettes stymie tobacco control drive. *Deccan Herald*. https://www.deccanherald.com/national/cheap-chinese-cigarettes-706439.html

Kaufman, N. J., & Nichter, M. (2001). The marketing of tobacco to women: Global perspectives. In J. M. Samet & S.-Y. Yoon (Eds.), *Women and the tobacco epidemic: Challenges for the 21st century* (pp. 69–98). World Health Organization.

Kaur, J., & Jain, D. C. (2011). Tobacco control policies in India: Implementation and challenges. *Indian Journal of Public Health, 55*, 220–227. https://doi.org/10.4103/0019-557X.89941

Khojol, H. L. (2018, September 12). Tobacco use dips in Mizoram. *The Telegraph, Aizawl.* https://www.telegraphindia.com/states/north-east/tobacco-use-dips-in-mizoram/cid/1667978

Kim, A. E., Loomis, B. R., Busey, A. H., Farrelly, M. C., Willett, J. G., & Juster, H. R. (2013). Influence of retail cigarette advertising, price promotions, and retailer compliance on youth smoking-related attitudes and behaviours. *Journal of Public Health Management & Practice, 19*(6), E1–E9.

Kirchner, T. R., Cantrell, J., Anesetti-Rothermel, A., Ganz, O., Vallone, D. M., & Abrams, D. B. (2013). Geospatial exposure to point-of-sale tobacco: Real-time craving and smoking-cessation outcomes. *American Journal of Preventive Medicine, 45*(4), 379–385.

Kishore, K. (2014). Monograph of tobacco (*Nicotiana tabacum*). *Indian Journal of Drugs, 2*(1), 5–23.

Klesges, R. C., Sherrill-Mittleman, D., Ebbert, J. O., Talcott, G. W., & Debon, M. (2010). Tobacco use harm reduction, elimination, and escalation in a large military cohort. *American Journal of Public Health, 100*, 2487–2492. https://doi.org/10.2105/AJPH.2009.175091

Kotler, P., & Keller, K. L. (2012). *Marketing management* (14th ed.). Pearson Education.

Kulkarni, P. S., Parkar, S. R., Kate, N., Ninawe, K., & Limbachiya, R. (2018). Role of personality in tobacco smoking behaviour in corporate sector: A cross-sectional study. *Industrial Psychiatry Journal, 27*(1), 103–109. https://doi.org/10.4103/ipj.ipj_46_16

Ladusingh, L., Dhillon, P., & Narzary, P. K. (2017). Why do the youths in Northeast India use tobacco? *Journal of Environmental and Public Health, 2017*(2), 1–6. https://doi.org/10.1155/2017/1391253

Lal, P., Srinath, S., Goel, S., Singh, R. J., Sharma, D., Kumar, R., & Bera, O. (2015). Unravelling India's tobacco epidemic: Priorities and recommendations for the second round of Global Adult Tobacco Survey (GATS). *Global Health Promotion, 22*(2), 7–19. https://doi.org/10.1177/1757975914536914

Lal, P. G., Wilson, N. C., & Gupta, P. C. (2012). Attributable deaths from smoking in the last 100 years in India. *Current Science, 103*(9), 1085–1090.

Laldinliana. (2010). *Consumer behaviour in Mizoram: An empirical study* [Doctoral thesis, Mizoram University].

Lalfakzuali, C. (2014). *Tobacco dependence among Mizo adults: A psychological analysis* [Doctoral thesis, Mizoram University].

Lalmuansangkimi, C. (2015). A reflection on the emergence of print and electronic media in Mizoram. *Global Media Journal – Indian Edition, 6*(1&2).

Lalramhluni, F. (2020). Regionalism and Mizo politics: A study of Mizoram People's Conference Party. *IOSR Journal of Humanities and Social Science, 25*(4), 47–54.

Lalremruati, C. (2019, March 27). Lungleiah 'Training on tobacco control for MJA and I&PR' neih a ni. *Directorate of Information & Public Relations, Government of Mizoram*. https://dipr.mizoram.gov.in/post/lungleiah-training-on-tobacco-control-for-mja-and-ipr-neih-a-ni

Lantz, P. M. (2018). Tobacco 21. *Contexts, 17*(1), 92–94. https://doi.org/10.1177/1536504218767129

Lee, W. B., & Dewhirst, T. (2011). Social marketing and tobacco control. In G. Hastings, C. Bryant, & K. Angus (Eds.), *The SAGE Handbook of Social Marketing* (pp. 391–404). SAGE Publications Ltd. https://doi.org/10.4135/9781446201008.n27

Legal Information Institute. (n.d.). 26 USC 5702: Definitions. *Cornell Law School*. Retrieved August 9, 2023, from https://www.law.cornell.edu/uscode/text/26/5702#:~:text=%E2%80%9CCigar%E2%80%9D%20means%20any%20roll%20of,substance%20not%20containing%20tobacco%2C%20and

Lejuez, C. W., Aklin, W., Bornovalova, M., & Moolchan, E. T. (2005). Differences in risk-taking propensity across inner-city adolescent ever- and never-smokers. *Nicotine & Tobacco Research, 7*(1), 71–79. https://doi.org/10.1080/14622200412331328484

Lejuez, C. W., Aklin, W. M., Jones, H. A., Richards, J. B., Strong, D. R., Kahler, C. W., & Read, J. P. (2003). The balloon analogue risk task (BART) differentiates smokers and non-smokers. *Experimental and Clinical Psychopharmacology, 11*(1), 26–33. https://doi.org/10.1037/1064-1297.11.1.26

Leventhal, A. M., Strong, D. R., Kirkpatrick, M. G., Unger, J. B., Sussman, S., Riggs, N. R., ... Audrain-McGovern, J. (2015). Association of electronic cigarette use with initiation of combustible tobacco product smoking in early adolescence. *Journal of the American Medical Association, 314*, 700–707.

Levin, M., & Stolberg, S. (1997, March 21). Tobacco company admits smoking leads to cancer. *Los Angeles Times*.

Lichtenberg, K. (2017). E-cigarettes: Current evidence and policy. *Missouri Medicine, 114*(5), 335–338. https://www.ncbi.nlm.nih.gov/pmc/articles/PMC6140188/

Loudon, D. C., & Bitta, A. J. D. (2002). *Consumer behaviour* (4th ed.). Tata McGraw-Hill.

MacFadyen, L., Hastings, G., & MacKintosh, A. M. (2001). Cross-sectional study of young people's awareness of and involvement with tobacco marketing. *BMJ (Clinical Research Edition), 322*(7285), 513–517. https://doi.org/10.1136/bmj.322.7285.513

Maggs, J. (1997). Alcohol use and binge drinking as goal-directed action during the transition to postsecondary education. In S. John, L. M. Jennifer, & H. Klaus (Eds.), *Health risks and developmental transitions during adolescence* (pp. 345–371). Cambridge University Press.

Mahanta, J., Chetia, M., Hazarika, N. C., Narain, K., & Sharma, S. K. (1998). Toxicity of tuibur, a unique form of tobacco smoke extract used in Mizoram, India. *Current Science*, *75*(4), 381–384.

Mamtani, R., Cheema, S., Sheikh, J., Mulla, A. A., Lowenfels, A., & Maisonneuve, P. (2017). Cancer risk in waterpipe smokers: A meta-analysis. *International Journal of Public Health*, *62*, 73. https://doi.org/10.1007/s00038-016-0856-2

Mansour, A. Y., & Bakhsh. (2017). Factors affecting the perceived effectiveness of pictorial health warnings on cigarette packages in Gulf countries: A cross-sectional study. *Tobacco Use Insights*, *10*, 1–7. https://doi.org/10.1177/1179173X17698462

Mathew, J. L., Patwari, A. K., Gupta, P., Shah, D., Gera, T., Gogia, S., ... & Kumar, R. (2011). Acute respiratory infection and pneumonia in India: A systematic review of literature for advocacy and action: UNICEF-PHFI series on newborn and child health, India. *Indian Pediatrics*, *48*, 191–218. PMID: 21478555

Mathur, C., Stigler, M. H., Erickson, D. J., Perry, C. L., Finnegan Jr., J. R., Arora, M., & Reddy, K. S. (2014). Change in tobacco use over time in urban Indian youth: The moderating role of socioeconomic status. *Health Education & Behavior*, *41*(2), 121–126. https://doi.org/10.1177/1090198113478817

McAlister, A., Perry, C. L., & Macoby, N. (1979). Adolescent smoking: Onset and prevention. *Pediatrics*, *63*, 650–658.

McKay, A. J., Patel, R. K. K., & Majeed, A. (2015). Strategies for tobacco control in India: A systematic review. *PLOS ONE*, *10*(4), e0122610. https://doi.org/10.1371/journal.pone.0122610

Mini, G. K., Sarma, P. S., & Thankappan, K. R. (2014). Pattern of tobacco use and its correlates among older adults in India. *Asian Pacific Journal of Cancer Prevention*, *15*(15), 6195–6198.

Ministry of Health & Family Welfare. (2018). *Global Adult Tobacco Survey Fact Sheet Mizoram 2016–17*. Government of India. https://tmc.gov.in/images/act/Mizoram-GATS2-India-StateFactsheet-Countryspecific-latest-v13.pdf

Ministry of Health & Family Welfare. (n.d.). *About NTCC*. Government of India. https://mohfw.gov.in/sites/default/files/About%20NTCC.pdf

Mishra, A., Arora, M., Stigler, M. H., Komro, K. A., Lytle, L. A., Reddy, K. S., & Perry, C. L. (2005). Indian youth speak about tobacco: Results of focus group discussions with school students. *Health Education & Behavior*, *32*(3), 363–379. https://doi.org/10.1177/1090198104272332

Mishra, G. A., Pimple, A. S., & Shastri, S. S. (2012). An overview of the tobacco problem in India. *Indian Journal of Medical and Paediatric Oncology*, *33*(3), 139–145. https://doi.org/10.4103/0971-5851.103139

Mishra, S., Joseph, R. A., Gupta, P. C., Pezzack, B., Ram, F., Sinha, D. N., Dikshit, R., Patra, J., & Jha, P. (2016). Trends in bidi and cigarette smoking in India from 1998 to 2015, by age, gender and education. *BMJ Global Health, 1*(1), e000005. https://doi.org/10.1136/bmjgh-2015-000005

Mizoram Pradesh Congress Committee. (2016). *Short report of Mizoram State Tobacco Control Society from April 2014 to June 2016*. http://www.mpccmizoram.org/wp-content/uploads/2016/08/Report-of-MSTCS.docx

Mizoram State National Informatics Centre. (n.d.). *Young Mizo Association*. http://mizoram.nic.in/more/yma.htm

Mizoram State Tobacco Control Society. (2013). *Children's day 2013*. https://tobaccocontrol.mizoram.gov.in/post/childrens-day-2013

Mizoram State Tobacco Control Society. (2018). *About the department*. https://tobaccocontrol.mizoram.gov.in/page/about-the-department

Mohan, P., & Lando, H. A. (2016). Oral tobacco and mortality in India. *Indian Journal of Clinical Medicine, 7*, 5–12. https://doi.org/10.4137/IJCM.S25889

Mohan, P., Lando, H. A., & Paneer, S. (2018). Assessment of tobacco consumption and control in India. *Indian Journal of Clinical Medicine, 9*, 1–8. https://doi.org/10.1177/1179916118759289

Mohan, S., Mini, G. K., & Thankappan, K. R. (2013). High knowledge of Framework Convention on Tobacco Control provisions among local government representatives does not translate into effective implementation: Findings from Kerala, India. *Public Health, 127*(2), 178–181. https://doi.org/10.1016/j.puhe.2012.11.018

Moodie, C., Hastings, G., Thomas, J., Stead, M., Angus, K., & Bauld, L. (2011). *Protocol for plain tobacco packaging: A systematic review*. https://www.researchgate.net/publication/267826564_Protocol_for_Plain_Tobacco_Packaging_A_Systematic_Review

Moodie, C., Stead, M., Bauld, L., McNeill, A., Angus, K., Hinds, K., ... O'Mara-Eves, A. (2012). *Plain tobacco packaging: A systematic review*. Public Health Research Consortium.

Murukutla, N., Turk, T., Prasad, C. V., Saradhi, R., Kaur, J., Gupta, S., ... Wakefield, M. (2012). Results of a national mass media campaign in India to warn against the dangers of smokeless tobacco consumption. *Tobacco Control, 21*(1), 12–17. https://doi.org/10.1136/tc.2010.039438

National Cancer Institute. (2008). *The role of the media in promoting and reducing tobacco use* (Tobacco Control Monograph No. 19). U.S. Department of Health and Human Services, National Institutes of Health, National Cancer Institute.

National Informatics Centre. (n.d.). *Mizo Hmeichhe Insuihkhawm Pawl*. NIC, Mizoram. Retrieved May 19, 2019, from http://www.mizoram.nic.in/more/mhip.htm

National Sample Survey Organization. (1998). A note on consumption of tobacco in India, NSS 50th Round (1993–1994). *A Journal of the National Sample Survey Organisation, 21*(3), 69–100.

Nayan, S. (2018). A brief report on excavation and new discoveries at Vangchhia, Mizoram. *Archaeological Survey of India, Aizawl Circle.* (Sessions 2015–16 & 2017–18).

Nayan, S., & Singh, M. J. (2022). Menhirs and petroglyphs of Vangchhia. *Indian Journal of Archaeology, 7*(1), 53–84. https://www.ijarch.org

Nguyen, D., & Aamodt, G. (2019). *The history of E-cigarettes*. Retrieved July 27, 2019, from https://www.dentalcare.com/en-us/professional-education/ce-courses/ce451/the-history-of-e-cigarettes

Nichter, M., & Muramoto, M. (2010). Project Quit Tobacco International: Laying the groundwork for tobacco cessation in low- and middle-income countries. *Asia-Pacific Journal of Public Health, 22*(3), 181S–188S. https://doi.org/10.1177/1010539510373023

Norcini, J. G. (2008). Native wildflower seed production: An alternative commodity for tobacco growers. In A. Hussain & N. Karamakar (Eds.), *Tobacco consumption: Socio-economic implications* (pp. 199–217). The Icfai University Press.

Northeast Today. (2015, December 14). Mizoram has the highest rate of tobacco consumption in India. Retrieved May 21, 2019, from https://www.northeasttoday.in/mizoram-has-the-highest-rate-of-tobacco-consumption-in-india/

Northeast Today. (2015, March 16). Highest death in Mizoram due to cancer. Retrieved May 17, 2019, from https://www.northeasttoday.in/highest-death-in-mizoram-due-to-cancer/

Novotny, T. E., & Mamudu, H. M. (2008). *Progression of tobacco control policies: Lessons from the United States and implications for global action* (Health, Nutrition and Population (HNP) Discussion Paper). The International Bank for Reconstruction and Development / The World Bank.

O'Malley, P., & Johnston, L. (2002). Epidemiology of alcohol and other drug use among American college students. *Journal of Studies on Alcohol, 14*, 23–39.

Office of Medical Applications. (1986). Health applications of smokeless tobacco use. *Journal of the American Medical Association, 255*, 1045–1048.

Pachuau, J. L. K., & Schendel, W. V. (2015). *The camera as witness: A social history of Mizoram, Northeast India*. Cambridge University Press.

Pachuau, M. (2008). *Hand-picked tales from Mizoram*. Writers Workshop.

PahrüPou, Z. K. (2017, March 23). Church and tobacco. *The Morung Express*, BTC, Pfutsero. http://morungexpress.com/church-and-tobacco/

Pain, A. K. (2008). Tobacco in medicine: A historical perspective. In A. Hussain & N. Karamakar (Eds.), *Tobacco consumption: Socio-economic implications* (pp. 28–33). The Icfai University Press.

Patja, K., Hakala, S. M., Bostrom, G., Nordgren, P., & Haglund, M. (2009). Trends of tobacco use in Sweden and Finland: Do differences in tobacco policy relate to tobacco use? *Scandinavian Journal of Public Health, 37*, 153–160. https://doi.org/10.1177/1403494808100277

Pearson, J. L., Richardson, A., Niaura, R. S., Vallone, D. M., & Abrams, D. B. (2012). e-Cigarette awareness, use, and harm perceptions in US adults. *American Journal of Public Health, 102*, 1758–1766.

Pettigrew, S., Santos, J. A., Miller, M., Raj, T. S., Jun, M., Morelli, G., & Jones, A. (2023). E-cigarettes: A continuing public health challenge in India despite comprehensive bans. *Preventive Medicine Reports, 31*, 102108. https://doi.org/10.1016/j.pmedr.2022.102108

Petty, R. E., & Cacioppo, J. T. (1983). Central and peripheral routes to persuasion: Application to advertising. In L. Percy & A. Woodside (Eds.), *Advertising and consumer psychology*. Lexington Books.

Petty, R. E., & Cacioppo, J. T. (1986). Elaboration likelihood model of persuasion. *Advances in Experimental Social Psychology, 19*, 123–193.

Pierce, J. P., & Gilpin, E. (1995). A historical analysis of tobacco marketing and the uptake of smoking by youth in the United States: 1890–1977. *Health Psychology, 14*(6), 500–508.

Planning & Programme Implementation Department. (2018). *Economic survey 2017–18*. Government of Mizoram, Research & Development Branch.

Planning & Programme Implementation Department. (2023). *Economic survey of Mizoram (2022–2023)*. Government of Mizoram, Research & Development Branch.

Press Information Bureau. (2025, May 20). Mizoram achieves full functional literacy. *Press Information Bureau, Government of India*. Retrieved May 27, 2025, from https://www.pib.gov.in/PressReleasePage.aspx?PRID=2130080

Prochaska, J. O., & DiClemente, C. C. (1984). *The transtheoretical approach: Crossing the traditional boundaries of therapy*. Dow-Jones/Irwin.

Prochaska, J. O., & DiClemente, C. C. (1986). Toward a comprehensive model of change. In W. R. Miller & N. Heather (Eds.), *Treating addictive behaviours: Processes of change* (pp. 3–27). Plenum Press.

Psychology Today. (2019). Nicotine. Retrieved July 04, 2019, from https://www.psychologytoday.com/au/conditions/nicotine

Puri, D. (2025, March 18). Despite ban, e-cigarettes readily available in India: Doctors concerned over rising popularity of vaping among Indian youth. *Media India*. Retrieved May 30, 2025, from https://mediaindia.eu/society/despite-ban-e-cigarettes-readily-available-in-india/

Ralte, L. (2016). *Religiosity and attire: A study on buying behaviour among the Mizo* (M. Phil Thesis). Department of Commerce, Mizoram University.

Randall, V. R. (1999). History of tobacco. Boston University Medical Center, Community Outreach Health Information System. Retrieved July 6, 2019, from https://academic.udayton.edu/health/syllabi/tobacco/history.htm

Rath, S. P. (2010). *Curbing consumption of oral intoxicants through social marketing and advertising: A strategic approach for the state of Orissa* (Doctoral Thesis). School of Management, KIIT University. https://shodhganga.inflibnet.ac.in/handle/10603/146075#

Raute, L. J., Pednekar, M. S., & Gupta, P. C. (2009). Pictorial health warnings on cigarette packs: A population based study findings from India. *Tobacco Use Insights, 2*, 11–16. https://doi.org/10.7860/JCDR/2015/14528.6748

Rawat, M. (2019, September 19). Explained: What are e-cigarettes? Why did the govt ban them? *India Today*. https://www.indiatoday.in/india/story/what-are-e-cigarettes-why-have-they-been-banned-1600452-2019-09-18

Rawat, R., Gouda, J., & Shekhar, C. (2015). Smokeless tobacco use among adult males in India and selected states: Assessment of education and occupation linkages. *Journal of Human Behavior in the Social Environment, 26*(2). https://doi.org/10.1080/10911359.2015.1083507

Reddy, K. S., & Gupta, P. C. (2004). *Report on tobacco control in India*. Ministry of Health and Family Welfare, Government of India.

Reddy, K. S., Chaloupka, F. J., Arora, M., Panda, R., Mathu, M. R., Samet, J., … Bettcher, D. (2010). A prioritized research agenda for prevention and control of noncommunicable diseases. Paper 1: Research priorities in tobacco control. *Working paper series*. World Health Organization. https://apps.who.int/iris/handle/10665/44447

Reddy, K. S., Yadav, A., Arora, M., & Nazar, G. P. (2012). Integrating tobacco control into health and development agendas. *Tobacco Control, 21*, 281-286. https://doi.org/10.1136/tobaccocontrol-2011-050419

Ristache, R. M., & Rotărescu, V. S. (2015). Differences in decision making of adult smokers and non-smokers in risky situations. *Cognition, Brain, Behavior. An Interdisciplinary Journal, 19*(4), 313-325. https://doi.org/10.13140/RG.2.1.3857.2561

Robbins, H. (2010). *Comprehensive tobacco control guidance document*. Standards, Programs & Community Development Branch, Ministry of Health Promotion, Ontario, Canada.

Rogers, R. W. (1975). A protection motivation theory of fear appeals and attitude change. *Journal of Psychology, 91*, 93-114.

Sadik, T. (2014). Literature review: Traditional use of tobacco among indigenous peoples of North America. https://cottfn.com/wp-content/uploads/2015/11/TUT-Literature-Review.pdf

Schiffman, L. G., & Kanuk, L. L. (2007). *Consumer behaviour* (9th ed., pp. 35-36). Delhi: Pearson Education.

Schorling, J. B., Roach, J., Siegel, M., Baturka, N., Hunt, D. E., Guterbock, T. M., & Stewart, H. L. (1997). A trial of church-based smoking cessation interventions for rural African Americans. *Preventive Medicine, 26*, 92-101.

Seitz, C. M., Kabir, Z., Greiner, B. A., & Davoren, M. P. (2018). Student, faculty, and staff approval of university smoke/tobacco-free policies: An analysis of campus newspaper articles. *Tobacco Use Insights, 11*, 1-10. https://doi.org/10.1177/1179173X18765127

Shakespear, C.J. (1975). *The Lushei Kuki Clans. Tribal Research Institute,* Department of Art and Culture, Government of Mizoram. 11

Shimkhada, R., & Peabody, J. W. (2003). Tobacco control in India. *Bulletin of the World Health Organisation, 81*(1), 48-52.

Singh, A., & Ladusingh, L. (2014). Prevalence and determinants of tobacco use in India: Evidence from recent global adult tobacco survey data. *PLoS ONE, 9*(12), e114073. https://doi.org/10.1371/journal.pone.0114073

Sinha, D. N. (2006). Tobacco control in schools in India (India Global Youth Tobacco Survey & Global School Personnel Survey, 2006). Ministry of Health and Family Welfare, Government of India. http://www.searo.who.int/entity/noncommunicable_diseases/data/ind_gyts_report_2006.pdf

Sinlung. (2014, July 29). 67.2% population of Mizoram use tobacco. http://www.sinlung.com/2014/07/672-of-mizoram-population-use-tobacco.html

Slater, S. J., Chaloupka, F. J., Wakefield, M., Johnston, L. D., & O'Malley, P. M. (2007). The impact of retail cigarette marketing practices on youth smoking uptake. *Archives of Pediatrics and Adolescent Medicine, 161*(5), 440-445.

Smith, T. T., Schaff, M. B., Rupprecht, L. E., Schassburger, R. L., Buffalari, D. M., Murphy, S. E., … Donny, E. C. (2015). Effects of MAO inhibition and a combination of minor alkaloids, β-carbolines, and acetaldehyde on nicotine self-administration in adult male rats. *Drug and Alcohol Dependence, 155*, 243-252. https://www.ncbi.nlm.nih.gov/pmc/articles/PMC4581969/

Song, Y., Zhao, L., Palipudi, K. M., Asma, S., Morton, J., Talley, B., ... GATS Collaborative Group. (2013). Tracking MPOWER in 14 countries: Results from the Global Adult Tobacco Survey, 2008-2010. *Global Health Promotion, 23*(2), 24-37. https://doi.org/10.1177/1757975913501911

Soni, P. (2012). *Tobacco consumption patterns of school students in NCT of Delhi* (Doctoral Thesis). Department of Social Work, University of Delhi.

Soni, P., & Raut, D. K. (2012). Prevalence and pattern of tobacco consumption in India. *International Research Journal of Social Sciences, 1*(4), 36-43.

Stankevich, A. (2017). Explaining the consumer decision-making process: Critical literature review. *Journal of International Business Research and Marketing, 2*(6). https://doi.org/10.18775/jibrm.1849-8558.2015.26.3001

State Tobacco Control Cell. (2016). *Report for the Quarter Ending: 30th June 2016*. STCC, Mizoram.

Statista. (2021). Leading cigarette and tobacco companies in India as of June 2021, based on market capitalization. https://www.statista.com/statistics/944956/india-leading-cigarette-companies-based-on-market-capitalization/

Stead, M., Gordon, R., Angus, K., & McDermott, L. (2007). A systematic review on social marketing effectiveness. *Health Education, 107*(2), 126-191. https://doi.org/10.1108/09654280710731548

Stevenson, A. (2024). Why Mizoram is called Mizoram? Retrieved March 26, 2025, from https://www.ncesc.com/geographic-faq/why-mizoram-is-called-mizoram/?utm_source=chatgpt.com

Strand, J., Rothschild, M. L., & Nevin, J. R. (2004). "Place" and channels of distribution. *Social Marketing Quarterly, 10*(3-4), 8–13. https://doi.org/10.1080/15245000490892434

Suliankatchi Abdulkader, R., Sinha, D. N., Jeyashree, K., Rath, R., Gupta, P. C., Kannan, S., Agarwal, N., & Venugopal, D. (2019). Trends in tobacco consumption in India 1987–2016: Impact of the World Health Organisation Framework Convention on Tobacco Control. *International Journal of Public Health, 64*(6), 841–851. https://doi.org/10.1007/s00038-019-01252-x

Tata Institute of Social Sciences & Ministry of Health and Family Welfare. (2018). *Global Adult Tobacco Survey GATS 2 India 2016-17*. Tata Institute of Social Sciences, Mumbai and Ministry of Health and Family Welfare, Government of India.

Thakur, J. S., Prinja, S., Bhatnagar, N., Rana, S. K., Sinha, D. N., & Singh, P. K. (2015). Widespread inequalities in smoking and smokeless tobacco consumption across wealth quintiles in states of India: Need for targeted interventions. *Indian Journal of Medical Research*, *142*(6), 789–798.

Thankappan, K. R., & Thresia, C. U. (2007). Tobacco use & social status in Kerala. *Indian Journal of Medical Research*, *126*(4), 300–308.

Thavorn, K., & Chaiyakunapruk, N. (2008). A cost-effectiveness analysis of a community pharmacist-based smoking cessation programme in Thailand. *Tobacco Control*, *17*, 177–182.

The Economic Times. (May 29, 2015). The Mizoram state tobacco control society have bagged the prestigious World Health Organisation (WHO) award. *The Economic Times*. https://economictimes.indiatimes.com/news/politics-and-nation/mizoram-bags-prestigious-who-award-for-tobacco-control-programme/articleshow/47470374.cms

The Economic Times. (October 2, 2023). Possession of e-cigarettes violation of law: Health Ministry. Retrieved June 02, 2025, from https://economictimes.indiatimes.com/industry/healthcare/biotech/healthcare/possession-of-e-cigarettes-violation-of-law-health-ministry/articleshow/104108529.cms?utm_source=contentofinterest&utm_medium=text&utm_campaign=cppst

The Indian Express. (2010, May 27). Mizoram highest among states in tobacco consumption. *The Indian Express*. http://archive.indianexpress.com/news/mizoram-highest-among-states-in-tobacco-consumption/624438/

The Morung Express. (2017, November 27). Tobacco consumption in Mizoram declines. *The Morung Express*, Newmai News Network, Aizawl. http://morungexpress.com/tobacco-consumption-mizoram-declines/

The Morung Express. (2018, May 2). Mizoram kicks off world no tobacco month. *The Morung Express*, Newmai News Network, Aizawl. http://morungexpress.com/mizoram-kicks-off-world-no-tobacco-month/

The New India Express. (2020, May 10). Mizoram records 10 per cent drop in Infant Mortality Rate, J&K witness significant low. *The New India Express*. https://www.newindianexpress.com/good-news/2020/may/10/mizoram-records-10-per-cent-drop-in-infant-mortality-rate-jk-witness-significant-low-2141518.html

The Northeast Today. (2015). 10 Events that made headlines in Mizoram in 2015. *The Northeast Today*. Retrieved May 26, 2019, from https://thenortheasttoday.com/archive/10-events-that-made-headlines-in-mizoram-in-2015/

The Telegraph. (2012, November 15). CM lauds Mizoram journalists. *The Telegraph*, Aizawl. https://www.telegraphindia.com/states/north-east/cm-lauds-mizoram-journalists/cid/364989

The Tobacco Institute of India. (n.d.). Tobacco Production. Retrieved July 6, 2019, from https://www.tiionline.org/facts-sheets/tobacco-production/

Times of India. (2017, November 25). Northeast has highest tobacco users in 15-17 age group in country. *Times of India*, Guwahati. https://timesofindia.indiatimes.com/city/guwahati/northeast-has-highest-tobacco-users-in-15-17-age-group-in-country/articleshow/61791105.cms

Times of India. (2020, September 22). India Happiness Report 2020: Mizoram most happy state; Uttarakhand and Odisha at the bottom. *Times of India*. https://timesofindia.indiatimes.com/travel/travel-news/india-happiness-report-2020-mizoram-most-happy-state-uttarakhand-and-odisha-at-thebottom/as78252001.cms#:~:text=As%20per%20the%20report%2C%20Mizoram,10%20happiest%20states%20in%20India.

Tobacco Board. (2014). Tobacco Board activities. Ministry of Commerce & Industry, Government of India. Retrieved July 6, 2019, from https://tobaccoboard.com/bactivities.php

Tobacco Board. (2025). *Tobacco Board of India*. Ministry of Commerce & Industry, Government of India. Retrieved June 5, 2025, from https://tobaccoboard.com/indexeng.php

Tobacco-Free Life. (2016). History of tobacco. Retrieved July 6, 2019, from https://tobaccofreelife.org/tobacco/tobacco-history/

Tonsing, M. V., Ghatak, S., Lalrohlui, F., Kumar, N. S., & Zohmingthanga, J. (2018). Five year record on cancer incidence from a diagnostic centre in Mizoram, Northeast India. *Cancer Health Disparities*, *2*, e1–e15. https://doi.org/10.9777/chd.2018.10014

Transnational Institute. (2011). On the frontline of northeast India: Evaluating a decade of harm reduction in Manipur and Nagaland. *Drug Policy Briefing*, No. 35. https://www.tni.org/files/download/On%20the%20Frontline%20of%20Northeast%20India.pdf

Triandis, H. C. (1977). *Interpersonal behaviour*. Brooks/Cole Publishing Co.

Tribal Research Institute. (1993). *Mizo thilhlui thenkhat (Objects of Mizo antiquity)*. Directorate of Art & Culture, Government of Mizoram, Aizawl.

Turk, T., Murukutla, N., Gupta, S., Kaur, J., Mullin, S., Saradhi, R., & Chaturvedi, P. (2012). Using a smokeless tobacco control mass media campaign and other synergistic elements to address social inequalities in India. *Cancer Causes & Control*, *23*(1), 81–90. https://doi.org/10.1007/s10552-012-9903-3

Tyagi, P. (2022, December 3). Top ten fastest growing major state economies of India. *Business Today*. https://www.businesstoday.in/latest/economy/story/top-ten-fastest-growing-major-state-economies-of-india-355155-2022-12-03

U.S. National Cancer Institute & World Health Organization. (2016). *The economics of tobacco and tobacco control* (National Cancer Institute Tobacco Control Monograph 21). NIH Publication No. 16-CA-8029A. U.S. Department of Health and Human Services, National Institutes of Health, National Cancer Institute & World Health Organization.

Vanglaini. (2015, July 24). *MHIP-tevaihlolehgutkhakhapnazirtir*. Vanglaini. https://www.vanglaini.org/tualchhung/39691

Vanglaini. (2018, May 29). *Project Himnachungchangzirho*. Vanglaini. https://www.vanglaini.org/tualchhung/85002

Vanglaini. (2018, September 12). *Mizoram state anti-tobacco day hmang*. Vanglaini. https://www.vanglaini.org/tualchhung/88808

Vanlalngilneii, C., & Thamilarasan, M. (2016). Tobacco, gender roles, and cancer in the Mizo society: How gender determines cancer prevalence through gendered view of tobacco. *Mizoram University Journal of Humanities & Social Sciences, 2*(2), 161–171.

Varshney, V. (2015, July 4). Mizoram's malignancy: Cancer gnawing at the northeast state. *Down To Earth*. https://www.downtoearth.org.in/news/mizorams-malignancy-12966

Vartiainen, E., Pallonen, U., McAlister, A. L., & Puska, P. (1990). Eight-year follow-up results of an adolescent smoking prevention program: The North Karelia project. *American Journal of Public Health, 80*, 78–79.

Wakefield, M., Germain, D., Durkin, S., & Henriksen, L. (2006). An experimental study of effects on schoolchildren of exposure to point-of-sale cigarette advertising and pack displays. *Health Education Research, 21*, 338–347. https://doi.org/10.1093/her/cyl005

Wales, M. (2008). Searching for alternative crops to replace or enhance tobacco in Canada. In A. Hussain & N. Karamakar (Eds.), *Tobacco consumption: Socio-economic implications* (pp. 163–198). The Icfai University Press.

WebIndia123. (2010, June 20). Mizo women embark on anti-gutkha campaign. *WebIndia123*. https://news.webindia123.com/news/articles/india/20100620/1530740.html

Widome, R., Brock, B., Noble, P., & Forster, J. L. (2012). The relationship of point-of-sale tobacco advertising and neighborhood characteristics to underage sales of tobacco. *Evaluation & the Health Professions, 35*(3), 331–345. https://doi.org/10.1177/0163278712447624

World Health Organisation India. (n.d.). Tobacco. Retrieved November 9, 2018, from http://www.searo.who.int/india/topics/tobacco/en/

World Health Organization. (1983). *Guidelines for the conduct of tobacco smoking surveys for the general population* (Document WHO/SMO/83.4). Geneva, Switzerland: Author.

World Health Organization. (1999). *Meeting report. Meeting on Tobacco and Religion*. Division of Noncommunicable Diseases, Tobacco Free Initiative. Geneva, Switzerland. Retrieved May 15, 2019, from https://www.who.int/tobacco/media/en/religioneng.doc

World Health Organization. (2003). *WHO Framework Convention on Tobacco Control*. Geneva, Switzerland: Author.

World Health Organization. (2008a). *WHO report on the global tobacco epidemic, 2008: The MPOWER package*. Retrieved March 28, 2019, from https://www.who.int/tobacco/mpower/en/

World Health Organization. (2008b). *Elaboration of guidelines for implementation of Article 13 of the Convention* (Third session of the Conference of the Parties to the WHO Framework Convention on Tobacco Control, Durban, South Africa, 17–22 November 2008). Retrieved January 14, 2019, from http://apps.who.int/gb/fctc/PDF/cop3/FCTC_COP3_9-en.pdf

World Health Organization. (2009a). *Tobacco*. Retrieved July 7, 2019, from https://www.who.int/nmh/publications/fact_sheet_tobacco_en.pdf

World Health Organization. (2009b). *Unhealthy diets & physical inactivity*. NMH Fact Sheet June 2009. Retrieved July 20, 2019, from https://www.who.int/nmh/publications/fact_sheet_diet_en.pdf

World Health Organization. (2011). *WHO report on the global tobacco epidemic: Warning about the dangers of tobacco*. Retrieved May 16, 2016, from http://www.who.int/tobacco/global_report/2011/en/

World Health Organization. (2016). *Plain packaging of tobacco products: Evidence, design and implementation*. Geneva, Switzerland: Author.

World Health Organization. (2018a, March 22). Smoking and tuberculosis: A dangerous combination [News release]. Retrieved August 13, 2023, from https://www.who.int/europe/news/item/22-03-2018-smoking-and-tuberculosis-a-dangerous-combination

World Health Organization. (2018b). *Global adult tobacco survey fact sheet India 2016-17*. Retrieved November 18, 2018, from http://www.who.int/tobacco/surveillance/survey/gats/GATS_India_2016-17_FactSheet.pdf

World Health Organization. (2019a). *Tobacco key facts*. Retrieved July 6, 2019, from http://www.who.int/news-room/fact-sheets/detail/tobacco

World Health Organization. (2019b, February 27). *Primary health care*. Retrieved July 25, 2019, from https://www.who.int/news-room/fact-sheets/detail/primary-health-care

World Health Organization. (2021). *WHO report on the global tobacco epidemic 2021: Addressing new and emerging products*. Geneva, Switzerland: Author.

World Health Organization. (n.d.). Factors affecting consumer behaviour of purchasing tobacco products. Retrieved August 8, 2019, from https://www.who.int/tobacco/economics/2_1ffactorsaffectingconsumerbehaviour.pdf

World Health Organization. (n.d.). WHO global health days. Retrieved November 20, 2018, from http://www.who.int/campaigns/no-tobacco-day/2017/event/en/

Yadav, A. (2019, July 23). Smoking e-cigarettes is more injurious to health. *The Hindu*. https://www.thehindu.com/opinion/op-ed/smoking-e-cigarettes-is-more-injurious-to-health/article28658584.ece

Yaya, S., Bishwajit, G., Shah, V., & Ekholuenetale, M. (2017). Socioeconomic disparities in smoking behaviour and early smoking initiation among men in Malawi. *Tobacco Use Insights, 10*, 1–7. https://doi.org/10.1177/1179173X17726297

Young Mizo Association. (2012, October 29). A brief history about Young Mizo Association. Retrieved May 11, 2019, from https://www.facebook.com/201229090011864/posts/a-brief-history-of-young-mizo-associationyoung-mizo-association-yma-as-it-is-pop/201254130009360/

Zate, H. (2017). Mizo Zirlai Pawl (Mizo Students' Association). Retrieved May 26, 2019, from https://mizoramtourism.org/other/mizo-zirlai-pawl-mizo-students-association

Zatoński, M., & Stokłosa, M. (2017). Report from the seminar on the past, present, and future of tobacco control, Harvard University, Department of the History of Science, Cambridge, Massachusetts, October 2016. *Journal of Health Inequalities, 3*(1), 16–23. https://doi.org/10.5114/jhi.2017.69160

Zomuanthanga, J. C. (2008). The civil society in Mizoram: A study of the church and YMA. In J. K. Patnaik (Ed.), *Peace and Development in Mizoram: Role of the State and Civil Society* (pp. xx–xx). Proceedings of the NEC sponsored National Seminar organised by Department of Political Science, Mizoram University, Aizawl (2nd–3rd November, 2007).

Zonet Chanchin Thar. (2018, September 11). Mizoram state anti-tobacco day 2018 chuvawiin khan Aijal Club Conference Hall-ah Transport Minister, Pu John Rotluangliana hovahman a ni. Retrieved May 25, 2019, from http://www.zonet.in/mizoram-state-anti-tobacco-day-2018-chu-vawiin-khan-aijal-club-conference-hall-ah-transport-minister-pu-john-rotluangliana-hova-hman-a-ni/

Zorammuana, K. (2010). *Civil society and state administration: Dimensions and interactions* (Post Graduate Dissertation). Department of Public Administration, Mizoram University, Aizawl, Mizoram.

Zotinkhuma, A. (2018, December 7). Ginger group shows the way. *The Hindu Business Line*. https://www.thehindubusinessline.com/blink/cover/ginger-group-shows-the-way/article256876

* * * *

Glossary of Acronyms and Abbreviations

4P	:	Product, Price, Place & Promotion or Proposition, Perception, Platform & Persuasion. Also popularly known marketing mix elements which is used in planning marketing strategy.
ACT	:	Action Council against Tobacco, an NGO working towards tobacco control in India.
AIDS	:	Acquired Immunodeficiency Syndrome
ASI	:	Archaeological Survey of India
ATC	:	Active Tobacco Consumers
CAGR	:	Compound Annual Growth Rate
CASAA	:	Consumer Advocates for Smoke-free Alternatives Association
CBO	:	Community-Based Organisation
CDC	:	U.S. Centers for Disease Control and Prevention
CEO	:	Chief Executive Officer
CID	:	Crime Investigation Department
CMO	:	Chief Medical Officer
COTPA	:	Cigarettes and Other Tobacco Products (Prohibition of Advertisement and Regulation of Trade and Commerce, Production, Supply and Distribution) Act, 2003
CPHA	:	Canadian Public Health Association

CPSC	:	Community-Pharmacist-Based Smoking Cessation
CSO	:	Central Statistical Office
CTCP	:	California's Tobacco Control Program
CYMA	:	Central Young Mizo Association
DDG	:	Deputy Director General
DES	:	Department of Economics and Statistics
DGP	:	Director General of Police
DIG	:	Deputy Inspector General
DRS	:	Demand Reduction Service
DTCC	:	District Tobacco Control Cells
e-cigarettes	:	Electronic Cigarettes
EFCI	:	Evangelical Free Church of India
EI	:	Educational Institutions
ENDS	:	Electronic Nicotine Delivery Systems
ETS	:	Environmental Tobacco Smoke
FCTC	:	Framework Convention on Tobacco Control
FCV	:	Flue-Cured Virginia
GATS	:	Global Adult Tobacco Survey
GHPS	:	Global Health Professional Survey
GOI	:	Government of India
GOM	:	Government of Mizoram
GSDP	:	Gross State Domestic Product
GSPS	:	Global School Personnel Survey
GTSS	:	Global Tobacco Surveillance System
GYTS	:	Global Youth Tobacco Survey
HFWD	:	Health and Family Welfare Department
HIV	:	Human Immunodeficiency Virus
HRIDAY-SHAN	:	Health Related Information Dissemination Amongst Youth-Students Health Action Network
I&PR	:	Information and Public Relations

IBEF : India Brand Equity Foundation

ICI : Independent Church of India

ICMR : Indian Council of Medical Research

ICTC : Indian Central Tobacco Committee

IEC : Information, Education and Communication

IQOS : I-Quit-Ordinary-Smoking. Line of heated tobacco and electronic cigarette products manufactured by Philip Morris International (PMI)

ISTH : Indian Society on Tobacco and Health

ISTHMC : Indian Society on Tobacco & Health (Mizoram Chapter)

ITC : ITC was originally an acronym for Imperial Tobacco Company of India Limited. It was renamed as India Tobacco Company Limited in 1970 and again abbreviated as ITC Ltd in 1974.

LAMPs : Legal Age Meeting Points. Used by some tobacco companies to refer places like bars and nightclubs where they can find prospective customers who are 18 and above.

LIKBK : Lairam Jesus Christ Baptist Church

MADAT : Mizoram against Drugs, Alcohol and Tobacco

MAOI : Monoamine oxidase inhibitors

MHFW : Ministry of Health and Family Welfare

MHIP : Mizo Hmeichhe Insuihkhawm Pawl

MJA : Mizoram Journalist Association

MKHC : Mizoram Kohhran Hruaitute Committee

MLTP : Mizoram Liquor Total Prohibition

MP : Member of Parliament

MPCC : Mizoram Pradesh Congress Committee

MPOWER : MPOWER stands for M : monitor tobacco use and prevention policies; P : protect people from tobacco smoke; O : offer help to quit tobacco smoking; W :

		warn about the dangers of tobacco; E : enforce bans on tobacco advertising, promotion and sponsorship; and R : raise taxes on tobacco
MSOA	:	Mizoram State Olympic Association
MSTC	:	Mizoram State Tobacco Control Society
MSTCP	:	Mizoram State Tobacco Control Programme
MSTCP	:	Mizoram State Tobacco Control Programme
MSTCS	:	Mizoram State Tobacco Control Society
MUP	:	Mizoram Upa Pawl (Zoram Aged Person Association). An NGO in Mizoram founded in the year 1960.
MZP	:	Mizo Zirlai Pawl (Mizo Student Union)
NCCP	:	National Cancer Control Programme
NER	:	North-eastern Region
NFHS	:	National Family Health Survey
NGO	:	Non-governmental Organisations
NITI Aayog	:	National Institution for Transforming India
NSSO	:	National Sample Survey Organisation
NTC	:	Non-Tobacco Consumers
NTCC	:	National Tobacco Control Cell
NTCP	:	National Tobacco Control Programme
PBCR	:	Population Based Cancer Registries
PECA	:	Prohibition of Electronic Cigarettes Act, 2019
PHW	:	Pictorial Health Warning. The mandatory warnings displayed along with images on tobacco packaging to discourage tobacco consumption
PMI	:	Philip Morris International
PPID	:	Planning and Programme Implementation Department
PTC	:	Past Tobacco Consumers

RTI International	:	Research Triangle Institute. It is a nonprofit organisation headquartered in the Research Triangle Park in North Carolina, USA
SHS	:	Second Hand Smoke
SLT	:	Smokeless Tobacco
SRS	:	Supply Reduction Service
STCC	:	State Tobacco Control Cell
TCC	:	Tobacco Control Cell
TEPC	:	Tobacco Export Promotion Council
TF	:	Tobacco-Free
TISS	:	Tata Institute of Social Sciences
TRA	:	Theory of Reasoned Action
TV	:	Tele Vision
US/USA	:	United States of America
VHAI	:	Voluntary Health Association of India
WHO	:	World Health Organisation
YMA	:	Young Mizo Association

Index

D

E

F

N

O

P

R

S

W

Y